PEARL HARBOR AIR RAID

The Japanese Attack on the U.S. Pacific Fleet, December 7, 1941

Nicholas A. Veronico

T0346579

STACKPOLE
BOOKS

Guilford, Connecticut

Published by Stackpole Books
An imprint of Globe Pequot
Trade Division of The Rowman & Littlefield Publishing Group, Inc.
4501 Forbes Boulevard, Suite 200, Lanham, Maryland 20706

Distributed by NATIONAL BOOK NETWORK

Cover design by Tessa Sweigert

British Library Cataloguing in Publication Information available

Library of Congress Cataloging-in-Publication Data

Names: Veronico, Nick, 1961- author.
Title: Pearl Harbor air raid : the Japanese attack on the U.S. Pacific Fleet,
    December 7, 1941 / Nicholas A. Veronico.
Other titles: Japanese attack on the U.S. Pacific Fleet, December 7, 1941
Description: Guilford, CT : Stackpole Books, [2017] | Includes
    bibliographical references.
Identifiers: LCCN 2016038945 (print) | LCCN 2016039147 (ebook) | ISBN
    9780811718387 (pbk. : alk. paper) | ISBN 9780811765497 (ebook)
Subjects: LCSH: Pearl Harbor (Hawaii), Attack on, 1941.
Classification: LCC D767.92 .V38 2017 (print) | LCC D767.92 (ebook) | DDC
    940.54/26693—dc23

CONTENTS

*For those who served and those
who made the ultimate sacrifice
on December 7, 1941.*

PREFACE

On the morning of December 7, 1941, the Japanese attacked the American naval and air bases on the island of Oahu, Territory of Hawaii. Bombs fell on the ships moored at the Pearl Harbor naval base, the Kaneohe Naval Air Station and the Marine Corps's Ewa Field, as well as the Army Air Force stations at Bellows, Hickam, and Wheeler Fields.

Within Pearl Harbor, Japanese carrier-based dive- and torpedo-bombers sank four battleships and damaged four others, and sent one minelayer and a training ship to the bottom. Three cruisers and three destroyers were also heavily damaged, some requiring more than two years to repair.

The American death toll in the attack reached 2,402 killed, with an additional 1,178 wounded. The largest loss of life was on board the battleship *Arizona* (BB-39), where 1,177 men perished. Serving on BB-39 were thirty-eight sets of brothers, of which twenty-three pairs along with a father and son lost their lives when the ship exploded. Civilians on the streets and in homes surrounding Pearl Harbor were impacted as well, with sixty-eight men, women, and children killed and thirty-five wounded. In comparison, losses of the attacking Japanese were light: twenty-nine aircraft, five midget submarines, and a total of sixty-four servicemen.

Simultaneous with the attack on Pearl Harbor, the Japanese assaulted American and British bases in the Philippines, Guam, Hong Kong, and Malaya and at Wake and Midway Islands. While the British, its colonies, and its Commonwealth protectorates (Australia, Canada, New Zealand, and South Africa) had been engaged in fighting the German, Italian, and Japanese—known as the Axis Powers—the Pearl Harbor attack brought total war to the United States of America.

The attack on Hawaii generated the cry to "Remember Pearl Harbor," which motivated men and women to sign up to serve in the military. Those not in uniform fought the battle on the home front, turning America into the "Arsenal of Democracy." Airplanes, ships, tanks, guns, ammunition, uniforms, boots, and every conceivable accoutrement needed to outfit a soldier to fight in any weather was made in America by those serving on the home front.

At the Pearl Harbor Naval Yard, hundreds of skilled technicians joined with Navy salvage crews and civilian contractors to return as many of the stricken ships to service as quickly as possible. The combined efforts returned all of the damaged ships to service except for the battleships *Arizona* and *Oklahoma* (BB-37) and the training ship *Utah* (BB-31/AG-16). Those repaired and returned to service would participate in a war that concluded with the Japanese surrender aboard the battleship *Missouri* (BB-63) on September 2, 1945. American military war dead totaled 407,300 servicemen and women.

In the years since the war, many books have been written about the Pearl Harbor attack. Some have claimed that U.S. government officials knew of the forthcoming Japanese action and let the attack go undefended in order to draw the United States into World War II. The true answer will never be known.

The Japanese attack lasted only two hours; thus, the number of photographs of the event is finite. *Pearl Harbor Air Raid* presents many familiar photos of the attack while many of the salvage images have never—or have only rarely—made it into print. The photos within this volume showcase the bravery of American servicemen and women in the face of a surprise enemy attack as well as the ingenuity of technicians who salvaged and returned ships of the Pacific Fleet to do battle with the enemy.

Nicholas A. Veronico
San Carlos, California

—

PROLOGUE:
MOVING FROM ONE WAR TO THE NEXT

Japan's quest for economic self-sufficiency and its efforts to expel the Allied powers from the Eastern Pacific and the Far East began shortly after the end of World War I. While Europe began to dress the wounds of World War I, Japan reaped the spoils of victory, acquiring the vanquished German territories in the Pacific, including the Caroline and Marshall island groups as well as the Marianas Islands (with the exception of Guam).

During World War I, the United States, Britain, and Japan each announced ship construction plans that essentially began a naval construction arms race. The United States had six battleships and six "battle cruisers" (faster than a battleship, yet more heavily armed than the typical cruiser, exemplified by ships such as HMS *Hood*) on the way, with the stated intention of building a fleet of fifty ships in these two classes. The British were planning on adding four battleships and four battle cruisers, while the Japanese announced plans for eight of each ship type.

In November 1921, the victorious powers gathered in Washington, D.C., to discuss limiting the numbers and sizes of warships in each nation's fleet. Known as the Washington Naval Arms Limitation Treaty of 1922, it set forth ship classes and sizes as well as a prohibition on the fortification of bases in the Pacific Ocean. America bargained away its right to supplement the defenses of Guam or the Philippines, while the British were restricted from fortifying its Pacific Ocean possessions, including Singapore and Hong Kong. Many of the battle cruisers then under construction were converted to aircraft carriers while other ships were scrapped and planned ships were not built. The treaty was ratified on August 17, 1923.

For seven years, Japan, the United States, and Great Britain managed a peaceful coexistence. At that time, the signatories to the Washington Naval Arms Limitation Treaty gathered in London to extend naval construction limitations. The outcome of the conference, known as the London Naval Treaty of 1930, was an agreement for a 10:10:6 ratio of heavy cruisers for the United States, Great Britain, and Japan and a 10:10:7 ratio for light cruisers and destroyers. The pact was ratified by the Japanese Diet, but the Imperial Navy believed the treaty's restrictions were too limiting and thought that the Diet had severely restricted its ability to wage war.

LIGHTING THE FUSE FOR A WORLD WAR

Although the Imperial Navy was limited in the size and number of ships for its fleet, the Imperial Japanese Army had other ambitions that did not require a flotilla of combat ships. On September 18, 1931, members of the Kwantung Army Group—an elite unit of the Imperial Japanese Army—blew up a South Manchurian railroad bridge at Mukden. Kwantung officers claimed Chinese partisans had blown up the bridge and attacked the army unit, using this incident to justify Japan's invasion of Manchuria.

In January 1932, the Imperial Japanese Army moved into Shanghai and, two months later, established its occupied territory in Manchuria as the state of "Manchuko" with former Chinese Emperor Henri Pu-Yi as head of the puppet government.

Four months later, on May 15, 1932, Japanese Prime Minister Tsuyoshi Inukai, who had attempted to halt the army's advance through Manchuria, paid for his actions with his life and was assassinated at his residence by nine soldiers. At the time, the Japanese prime minister and the ministers of the army and navy had equal power and equal access to the emperor. Inukai's death effectively ended party rule in Japan. The military replaced the government with a cabinet of eleven seats—eight military officers and three civilians—and appointed Adm. Makoto Saito as prime minister.

Having shifted the balance of power within Japan, the Kwantung Army marched into Inner Mongolia. Under the protests of the United States and the League of Nations, Japan refused to withdraw from China. In March 1933, the League issued the Lytton Report, which reiterated the call for a Japanese withdrawal, and an official statement refusing to recognize Manchuko as a legitimate government. Bowing to army pressure, Japan withdrew from the League of Nations. Following on the heels of Japan's withdrawal from the League, Germany gave notice on October 14, 1933, that it, too, was concluding its participation in the international organization.

One year later, in December 1934, Japan officially renounced its recognition of the Washington Naval Treaty and began a ship construction program in secret. Plans called for the construction of seven battleships of the *Yamato* class, each displacing an estimated 69,000 tons—larger than any other ship afloat, each with a main battery of nine 18-inch guns, capable of speeds in excess of 30 knots, and a range of 8,000 nautical miles at 18 knots. (Only three of the class were eventually completed, *Yamato, Mushashi*, and *Shinano*.)

Vowing to fight the enemy that is communism, Japan and Germany signed the Anti-Comintern Pact on November 26, 1936. One year later, Mussolini, joined the pact, thus forming the first vestiges of an Axis alliance.

From Manchuria, the Japanese Army marched into China on July 7, 1937, after a minor engagement near Peiping that became known as the Marco Polo Bridge Incident. The advance was brutal, with the army taking control of Shanghai and then butchering the citizens of Nanking in December 1937 when more than 200,000 lost their lives. The army's acquisition of Chinese lands ran into stiff opposition from Kuomintang and Chinese Communist partisans and, in May 1939, from the Russian army as well. During the border war with Russia along the Siberia, Manchuria, and Korea frontiers, the Japanese lost 500 aircraft and more than 150 pilots. The Russians stopped the Japanese advance, and in September both nations agreed to a ceasefire.

Japan's war with China was of little concern to Hitler, half a world away. Hitler faced only verbal opposition from Britain and France in March 1936 when his troops occupied and began fortifying the Rhineland. The west paid only lip service when Hitler proclaimed the union of Germany and Austria and shortly thereafter annexed the Sudetenland. Sensing that the allied nations of Western Europe did not have the resolve to stop Hitler with force,

the German *Wehrmacht* rolled across the border into Czechoslovakia on March 14, 1939, to occupy that once sovereign nation.

Watching the European balance of power swing toward Hitler's Germany, President Franklin D. Roosevelt could not allow America's isolationist policies to dictate foreign policy any longer. In an address to Congress on September 21, 1939, Roosevelt sought the repeal of the arms embargo that withheld American guns, ships, tanks, and planes from being sold to France and Great Britain. As Congress mulled over the possible implications of lifting the arms embargo, Germany and Russia forced America's legislative branch to act.

In the early morning hours of September 1, the German *Wehrmacht* rolled across the border into Poland. The *Luftwaffe* quickly gained air superiority and then turned its attention to supporting ground forces. This two-pronged, lightning-fast attack was dubbed the *Blitzkrieg*, and within twenty days, Poland's armed forces had been bombed and strafed into submission. Witnessing Hitler's decimation of Poland stirred the Congress of the United States to pass the Neutrality Act of November 4, 1939, which allowed America's defense industry to provide arms to allied countries on a "cash and carry" basis.

The spring of 1940 saw the U.S. Navy's Pacific Fleet sortie from the West Coast for maneuvers in Hawaiian waters. Once the exercise was completed, Roosevelt directed that the fleet remain stationed at Pearl Harbor as a deterrent to the Japanese. In theory, the Pacific Fleet would be seven sailing days closer to any Pacific conflict and would temper Japanese expansion plans to the south.

In Europe, Hitler invaded the Low Countries and France on May 10. France was quickly conquered, and by June 22, the Germans had divided the country into two sections, the northern half by the occupying *Wehrmacht* and the southern half by the Vichy-based government of Marshal Philippe Pétain. Japan quickly put pressure on the Vichy government to stem the flow of arms through France's Indochina colony to Chinese rebels led by Chiang Kai-shek. To ensure its position, Japan sent military units into northern French Indochina to police the border area. Seen as another expansionist move, Roosevelt swiftly reacted by cutting off Japan's supply of American oil, steel, and scrap iron—all necessary elements needed to wage war.

The following month, Fumimaro Konoe became the Japanese prime minister. The "Major Principles of Basic National Policy" were approved that solidified Japan's Asia-first policy. This called for an expansion to the south in an effort to gain territory that would help Japan's war economy become self-sufficient regardless of the consequences.

While Japan was planning its future, America was slowly taking steps to protect its shores. On September 2, an agreement was reached with the British whereby the island nation would receive fifty ex–World War I four-stack destroyers from America's mothball fleet in exchange for naval and air base leases in Newfoundland, Bermuda, and the Caribbean. By the end of the month, Japan, Germany, and Italy had signed the Tripartite Pact, solidifying their intent to cooperatively "maintain a new order . . . calculated to promote the mutual prosperity and welfare" of their nations. Within a week of signing, Japanese Prime Minister Konoe said in a newspaper interview: "If the United States refuses to understand the real intentions of Japan, Germany, and Italy and continues persistently its challenging attitude and acts . . . those powers will be forced to go to war. Japan is now endeavoring to adjust Russo-Japanese political and economic relations and will make every effort to reduce friction between Japan and Russia. Japan is now engaged in diplomatic maneuvers to induce Russia, Britain, and the United States to suspend their operations in assisting the Chiang regime."

DECEPTIVE RELATIONS
President Roosevelt received the Japanese Ambassador to the United States, Admiral Kichisaburo Nomura on February 14, 1941. The topic for discussion was the deterioration of Japanese-American relations, and Roosevelt suggested that the admiral frankly and openly discuss the troubles with Secretary of State Cordell Hull. Thus began a frustrating ten-month series of negotiations in which Secretary Hull attempted to ascertain Japan's "willingness and power to abandon its present doctrine of conquest by force" and to respect the sovereignty of all nations. While Hull sought the answer, Admiral Nomura continued to intimate that peace between both nations could be achieved.

Negotiations in Washington with the Japanese continued as the German navy began attacks against shipping farther and farther from the European coastline. The Germans were attempting a naval blockade of England using its limited fleet of U-boats and were enjoying much success. To increase aid to England while maintaining some semblance of neutrality, Roosevelt signed the Lend-Lease bill into law on March 11, 1941. The bill provided increased spending on armament for self-defense while enabling the

British to acquire vast amounts of shipping, aircraft, and other war materiél on a credit basis. Roosevelt stated that the materiél sent overseas kept the dictators from American shores while the nation continued to build a reserve of tanks, planes, and ships. American factories took on another lend-lease customer on June 22, 1941, when Hitler attacked Russia.

Admiral Nomura had engaged Secretary Hull in a number of meetings to discuss peace during the first half of the year. In July, Nomura and the Japanese foreign minister were repeatedly voicing their nation's desire for peace as the Japanese army marched into the southern areas of French Indochina. Unable to make any progress on a Japanese withdrawal from China, and faced with further expansion in Indochina, Roosevelt was forced to hit Japan where it hurt the most—in the wallet. The president signed an executive order on July 26, freezing all of Japan's financial assets in the United States and barring all import and export transactions involving Japanese interests.

While negotiations with Japan continued, in the Atlantic Ocean a number of incidents involving Germany were slowing drawing America closer to a two-front war. On September 4, *U-652* fired torpedoes at the U.S. Navy destroyer *Greer* (DD-145) while it was sailing to Argentia, Newfoundland. The *Greer* became the first U.S. naval vessel to attack the Germans when the ship dropped nineteen depth charges against *U-652*. Roosevelt used the encounter between the sub and American man o'war to rally the nation, claiming, "This was piracy—legally and morally. It was not the first nor the last act of piracy which the Nazi Government has committed against the American flag in this war." Less than a month later, the *Kearny* (DD-432) was escorting a convoy to England on the night of October 16, when three of her charges were torpedoed by a U-boat wolf pack. The following morning, *Kearny* was struck by a torpedo from *U-568* in the forward fire room. Thirty-three of *Kearny*'s crew lost their lives in the attack. The destroyer limped to Greenland for temporary repairs and eventually proceeded to an East Coast shipyard for restoration and refitting. Although *Kearny* was a ship in a neutral navy, the destroyer was escorting ships laden with cargo for a nation at war—justification to fire from the U-boat commander's perspective. From Roosevelt's perspective, the attack on the *Kearny* was reason enough to order the navy to "shoot on sight" any Axis vessel in U.S. waters or acting in a belligerent manner.

The peace process with the Japanese took a turn for the worse on October 16, when the Konoe cabinet toppled and was replaced by a cabinet headed by

Gen. Hideki Tojo. The Tojo cabinet expected America to make all concessions toward peace while Japan maintained its positions in French Indochina and mainland China. Major General Kiyofuku Okamoto expressed the new cabinet's position in a statement released October 17: "Despite the different view advanced on the Japanese-American question, our national policy for solution of the China affair and establishment of a common co-prosperity sphere in East Asia remains unaltered. For fulfillment of this national policy, this country has sought to reach an agreement of views with the U.S. by diplomatic means. There is, however, a limit to our concessions, and the negotiations may end in a break with the worst possible situation following." General Kiyofuku's statement was made as Admiral Nomura continued to present the hope of peace to Secretary Hull.

On November 3, Adm. Osami Nagano, chief of the Naval General Staff, and Admiral Isoroku Yamamoto finalized the plan of attack for Pearl Harbor. The emperor was aware of the plan to strike once the final ultimatum was delivered to the United States on December 7. This decision set in motion a number of deadlines, both diplomatic and military, that led to war. The United States Pacific Fleet was to be "rendered impotent" in Hawaii to afford the Japanese military time to invade the Philippines, the oil rich Dutch East Indies, the Malay Peninsula and the naval base at Singapore, and bolster its forces in the mandated islands.

The strike force, under the command of Vice Adm. Chuichi Nagumo, gathered in Hitokappu Bay near Etorfu Island in the Kurile Islands—six aircraft carriers (*Akagi, Hiryu, Kaga, Shokaku, Soryu,* and *Zuikaku*) with 423 combat planes aboard, two battleships (*Hiei* and *Kirishima*), and two heavy cruisers (*Chikuma* and *Tone*), plus the light cruiser *Abukma*, eleven destroyers (two, *Sazanami* and *Ushio*, would split off and shell the airbase at Midway Island), three submarines (*I-19, I-21,* and *I-23*) to serve as advance lookouts for the strike force, and eight tankers. An Advance Expeditionary Force of twenty-seven additional submarines would join in the attack, having sortied from Kure and Yokosuka between November 18 and 20. The subs refueled and resupplied at Kwajalein before proceeding on the mission. *I-26* left the pack to monitor shipping in the Aleutians, and *I-10* guarded the flank in the Samoa area. The remaining twenty-five I-boats set sail for Hawaiian waters, five to launch two-man midget submarines and the others to harass shipping. At 6 a.m. on November 26 (Tokyo time), the fleet sailed for Pearl Harbor following a northern course to avoid detection by commercial ships. If negotiations with the United States were successful, the attacking force could be recalled, and war avoided. If there was not a breakthrough in negotiations, the strike force would launch its aircraft at 6 a.m., one hour before sunrise, on Sunday morning, December 7 (Honolulu time; December 8 Tokyo time).

Unknown to Admiral Nomura, the fleet had sailed and diplomatic negotiations had been put on a strict timetable. Through diplomatic channels, the United States forwarded a document titled "Outline of Proposed Basis for Agreement between the United States and Japan" on November 26, calling for peace between the two nations. The document demanded Japan withdraw from Indochina and China, and once China was a sovereign nation, it called for the recognition of Chiang Kai-Shek's national government. The outline, which became known as the "November 26 Note," was an olive branch from the United States to Japan; in addition, it offered to release all frozen assets and to negotiate a reciprocal, most-favored-nation trade agreement.

Tokyo responded to Admiral Nomura with comments on the "November 26 Note" two days later. In dispatch No. 844, Tokyo informed the admiral and fellow diplomat Saburo Kurusu: "The United States has gone ahead and presented this humiliating proposal. This was quite unexpected and extremely regrettable. The Imperial Government can by no means use it as a basis for negotiations. Therefore, with a report of the view of the Imperial Government on this American proposal which I will send you in two or three days, the negotiations will be *de facto* ruptured. This is inevitable. However, I do not wish you to give the impression that the negotiations are broken off. Merely say to them that you are awaiting instructions and that although the opinions of your government are not yet clear to you, to your own way of thinking the Imperial Government has always made just claims and has borne great sacrifices for the sake of peace in the Pacific. Say that we have always demonstrated a long-suffering and conciliatory attitude, but that, on the other hand, the United States has been unbending, making it impossible for Japan to establish negotiations." In addition, the Japanese diplomats were informed that a response to the "November 26 Note" would be forthcoming, sent by cable in fourteen parts.

On the evening of December 6 in Washington, U.S. cryptanalysts had decoded and prepared the first thirteen parts of the message for distribution to the War Council that included the president, the secretaries of state, war, and the navy, and the chief

Imperial Japanese Navy Vice Admiral Chuichi Nagumo served as commander-in-chief of the First Air Fleet that carried out the Pearl Harbor attack. Well versed in surface tactics and torpedo attacks, when it came to airpower at this early stage of the war, Nagumo was an overly cautious commander. He refused his subordinates' recommendation for a third-wave attack on Pearl Harbor, which could have destroyed the fuel farm, caused more damage to the Navy Yard, and sent additional U.S. Navy ships to the bottom. He had considerable success in early 1942, but the losses at the Battle of Midway saw him recalled to Japan. Although Nagumo had a couple of additional commands, Allied numerical superiority overwhelmed his last command at the Battle of the Philippine Sea. He ended his life on July 6, 1944, on Saipan as the U.S. Marines were taking the island. NH63423

of staff and the chief of naval operations. What they read was a lengthy reiteration of Japan's reasons for conquest and why it should hold its territories. It blamed the United States for pushing both nations toward war. The last sentence of the thirteenth part read, "Therefore, viewed in its entirety, the Japanese Government regrets that it cannot accept the proposal [American proposal of November 26] as a basis of negotiations." The fourteenth part had been decoded and was in the process of being distributed at 8 a.m., on the morning of December 7. It read:

> Obviously it is the intention of the American Government to conspire with Great Britain and other countries to obstruct Japan's efforts toward the establishment of peace through the creation of a New Order in East Asia, and especially to preserve Anglo-American rights and interests by keeping Japan and China at war.
>
> The Japanese Government regrets to have to notify hereby the American Government

that in view of the attitude of the American Government it cannot but consider that it is impossible to reach an agreement through further negotiations.

Upon review, the message simply stated that negotiations could not proceed at this juncture. Nowhere did the message state that diplomatic relations between the two nations should be or were broken, nor did the message declare war upon the United States.

Although the War Council had read it, the Japanese delegation was having difficulties decoding and preparing the lengthy message for presentation to Secretary Hull. Along with the text, the cable instructed the diplomats to deliver the message at 1 p.m., Washington time, which was 7:30 a.m., Hawaiian time. (On December 7, 1941, there was a 5.5-hour time difference between Hawaii and Washington, D.C.) They did indeed set an appointment to deliver the message at 1 p.m., but later called and moved the appointment to 2 p.m.—unaware of the timing significance.

EARLY ON THE MORNING OF DECEMBER 7, 1941

While folks in Washington, D.C., slept during the early morning hours of December 7, 1941, events were unfolding in the waters around the Hawaiian island of Oahu.

At approximately 5 a.m., the cruisers *Tone* and *Chikuma* each launched a single Aichi E13A Jake floatplane—*Tone*'s plane to reconnoiter the Lahaina Roads anchorage on the west side of the island of Maui and *Chikuma*'s to scout Pearl Harbor. The Japanese had hoped to catch the American fleet anchored in the deep waters of the Lahaina anchorage. (Although the Allies' use of codenames for Japanese aircraft, such as Jake, was not introduced until mid-1942, they are today universally recognized and are used here for the ease of the reader.) *Tone*'s floatplane reported that no American naval vessels were in the deep-water anchorage at Lahaina while *Chikuma*'s aircraft sent a report of the number and types of aircraft in Pearl Harbor as well as a weather report back to the strike force.

The fleet is in port on October 30, 1941. The mouth of the harbor is seen at the top of the photo with Hickam Army Air Field to its left. The Pearl Harbor Navy Yard is adjacent to Hickam Field. The dock area and fuel farm are in the center left while ships are tied up to Battleship Row along Ford Island. Dominating the center of Ford Island is the naval air station, and five berths are located to the right of the island. NARA 80G-182874

Riding at anchor off the Honolulu shore are the aircraft carriers *Saratoga* (CV-3) and, at right, *Lexington* (CV-2). The Japanese had hoped to catch the U.S. Pacific Fleet's carriers at anchor on the morning of December 7, 1941, but fate intervened. *Saratoga* was undergoing refit at the Puget Sound Naval Yard in Washington state, *Lexington* was delivering reinforcement aircraft to Midway Island, and *Enterprise* (CV-6) was at sea returning from Wake Island. NARA

Pearl Harbor looking to the northwest with Battleship Row along Ford Island, the Pearl Harbor Navy Yard to the left, the supply base in the center, right, and piers of the submarine base protruding at the lower right. U.S. NAVAL HISTORY AND HERITAGE COMMAND NH54301

Looking down on the fuel farm and Submarine Base on October 13, 1941. Midway up the channel in the foreground, note the submarine tender *Holland* (AS-3) with submarines alongside and, just ahead of it, *Niagara* (PG-52) supporting a number of motor torpedo boats. This area of the base was spared during the December 7 attack. NARA 80G-182880

The Pearl Harbor Submarine Base was also home to the U.S. Pacific Fleet's headquarters. Adm. Husband E. Kimmel's office was on the top floor of the left side of the headquarters building, next to the submarine escape ascent tower. The Supply Depot can be seen in the upper center. The troop transport in the lower right is *Wharton* (AP-7), which earned three battle stars for service in the Pacific Theater. The battleship *Nevada* (BB-36) can be seen moored on Battleship Row in the upper left. NARA 80G-451125 / NH50266

The midget submariners were considered "Hero Gods" for having given their lives in the Pearl Harbor attack. From left, *I-20tou*'s crew of Akira Hiro-o (seated) and Yoshio Katayama (standing); *I-16tou*'s crew, Masaharu Yokoyama (seated, second from left) and Sadamu Kamita (standing, second from left); *I-22tou*'s Naoji Iwasa (seated, center) and Naokichi Sasaki (standing, center); *I-18tou*'s Shigemi Furuno (seated, second from right) with Shigenori Yokoyama (standing, second from right); and *I-24tou*'s Kazuo Sakamaki (seated, right) and Kiyoshi Inagaki (standing, right). BURL BURLINGAME COLLECTION VIA PARKS STEPHENSON

At 3:43 a.m., the U.S. Navy minesweeper *Condor* sighted a periscope off the entrance to Pearl Harbor. Twelve minutes later, this sighting was sent by signal light to the destroyer *Ward* (DD-139). The destroyer attempted to make contact with the submarine during the next couple of hours, but could not locate her. Lieutenant William W. Outerbridge, skipper of the *Ward*, understood the significance of a Japanese submarine lurking off the harbor's entrance, but did not report the phantom submarine sighting to higher command at the Pearl Harbor's Fourteenth Naval District.

At 6:30 a.m., the general stores issue ship *Antares* (AKS-3) arrived off Pearl Harbor towing a barge. While waiting for the harbor pilot to board the vessel and steer her though the narrow harbor entrance channel, a submarine was sighted off the *Antares*'s starboard side. Quickly notified, the *Ward* began the hunt while a PBY Catalina from Patrol Squadron Fourteen (VP-14) dropped a smoke pot to mark its location.

The *Ward* turned and ran down the submarine's track, opening up with her deck guns. A shot from the forward turret missed, but the mid-ships 4-inch/50-caliber gun put a round through the submarine's conning tower. As the *Ward* passed over the sub's location, she rolled a pattern of depth charges from her stern, ensuring that the as-yet-unidentified submarine went to the bottom. The *Ward* radioed the Fourteenth Naval District: "We have dropped depth charges upon subs operating the defensive sea area." Feeling this was not direct enough, two minutes later Outerbridge transmitted, "We have attacked, fired upon and dropped depth charges upon submarine operating in defensive sea area." It was 6:51 a.m.

During the *Ward*'s pursuit of the submarine at the mouth of Pearl Harbor, approximately 1,290 miles to the northwest, the 2,140-ton freighter SS *Cynthia Olson* was stopped by the Imperial Navy submarine *I-26*. The freighter was on charter to the U.S. Army carrying lumber for base construction on Oahu. A distress call was sent, and the crew boarded lifeboats while *I-26* began shelling the freighter with its 140mm deck gun. In spite of its buoyant cargo of lumber, the *Cynthia Olson* was sent to the bottom, and her crew was never heard from again.

Ward (DD-139) was a World War I–era 1,247-ton *Wickes*-class destroyer and is seen moored in the San Diego harbor, California, on August 14, 1920. In early 1941, *Ward* was sent to patrol Hawaiian waters and would make what many consider the opening shot of World War II when the crew of its number three gun put a shell through the conning tower of a Japanese midget submarine near the entrance to Pearl Harbor. Although many were unconvinced of the gun crew's accuracy, the *Ward*'s gun crew was vindicated when the submarine was found on August 28, 2002, with a hole in the conning tower at the connection to the hull. NH 106144

The gun crew from *Ward* was made up of reservists from the Minnesota Naval Reserve. Standing by the 4-inch/50-caliber gun amidships on the destroyer's starboard side are, from left: R. H. Knapp (boatswain's mate, second class), who served as the gun captain; gun pointer C. W. Fenton (seaman, first class); trainer Sea1c R. B. Nolde; number one loader Sea1c A. A. De Demagall; number two loader Sea1c D. W. Gruening; number three loader Sea1c J.A. Paick; number four loader Sea1c H. P. Flanagan; Gunner's Mate, third class E. J. Bakret; and sightsetter Coxswain K. C. J. Lasch. The historic gun was removed from the ship durin gan overhaul in 1942.
NH97446

Ensign Kazuo Sakamaki's *I-24tou* became lost and ran aground at Bellows Field. When the sun rose on December 8, it was quickly spotted and was attacked from the air. Although the attacks failed to destroy the midget submarine, they did free it from the coral and the sub floated into the surf line. It is seen after having been pulled from the waves and secured. Sakamaki became Prisoner of War No. 1, while his crewmate, Warrant Officer Kiyoshi Inagaki, drowned. U.S. NAVY

I-26 was a newly built type B1 submarine at the time of the Pearl Harbor attack. The submarine was commissioned on November 6, 1941, and was patrolling between Hawaii and the West Coast on the morning of December 7. The freighter SS *Cynthia Olson* crossed the marauding submarine's path moments before the Pearl Harbor attack began. U.S. NAVY

World War II's first victim of a submarine attack was the SS *Cynthia Olson*, on contract to the U.S. Army, carrying a load of lumber from Seattle, Washington, to Oahu. The freighter was shelled and sunk by the Imperial Japanese Navy submarine *I-26*. There were no survivors. USAHEC / SIGNAL CORPS PHOTO 140957

JAPANESE PEARL HARBOR ATTACK FLEET

Air Attacking Force
    Six Aircraft Carriers: *Akagi, Hiryu, Kaga, Shokaku, Soryu, Zuikaku*

Screening Unit (Rear Adm. Sentaro Omori)
    Light Cruiser: *Abukuma*
    Nine Destroyers: *Akigumo, Arare, Hamakaze, Isokaze, Kagero, Kasumi, Shiranuhi, Tanikaze, Urakaze*

Support Force (Rear Adm. Gunichi Mikawa)
    Two Battleships: *Hiei, Kirishima*
    Two Heavy Cruisers: *Chikuma, Tone*

Advance Submarine Screen Unit (Capt. Kijiro Imaizumi)
    Three Submarines: *I-19, I-21, I-23*

    Midget-Carrying Submarines and Type A Midget Submarines (*tou*)
        I-16 (commanded by Lt. Cmdr. Yamada Kaoryu)
        I-16tou crewed by Lt. Cmdr. Masaji Yokoyama and Warrant Officer (W.O.) Sadamu Uyeda

        I-18 (Cdr. Otani Kiyonori)
        I-18tou Lt. Cmdr. Shigemi Furuno and SubLt. Shigenori Yokoyama

        I-20 (Yamada Takashi)
        I-20tou Lt. Akira Hiroo and W.O. Yoshio Katayama

        I-22 (Cmdr. Ageta Kiyotake)
        I-22tou Cmdr. Naoji Iwasa and SubLt. Naokichi Sasaki

        I-24 (Cmdr. Hiroshi Hanabusa)
        I-24tou Ensign Kazuo Sakamaki and W.O. Kiyoshi Inagaki

First Submarine Group (Rear Adm. Tsutomu Sato)
    Stationed northeast of Oahu: *I-9, I-15, I-17, I-25*

Second Submarine Group (Rear Adm. Shigeaki Yamazaki)
    Stationed in the channels between Oahu and Kauai and Molokai: *I-1, I-2, I-3, I-4, I-5, I-6, I-7*

Third Submarine Group (Rear Adm. Shigeyoshi Miwa)
    Stationed south of Oahu: *I-8, I-68, I-69, I-70, I-71, I-72, I-73, I-74, I-75*

Support Ships
    1 Supply Unit
        Five Tankers: *Akebono Maru, Kenyo Maru, Kokuyo Maru, Kyokuto Maru, Shinkoku Maru*
    2 Supply Unit
        Three Tankers: *Nippon Maru, Toei Maru, Toho Maru*

Midway Neutralization Unit (Capt. Kaname Konishi)
    Two Destroyers: *Akebono, Ushio*

CHAPTER 1

"AIR RAID. THIS IS NO DRILL."

Sitting at the Opana Point aircraft warning station near the northern tip of Oahu on Sunday morning, December 7, were Privates Joseph Lockard and George Elliott. The men were manning an Army Signal Corps SCR-270 mobile radar that consisted of a trailer-mounted antenna, a truck carrying the 106MHz radar set, and a truck-mounted, gasoline-powered generator. These radar sets were a very new technology at the time, with the first training class for its operators having been held in April 1941. The SCR-270 was America's first long-range search radar, and the Opana Point site was one of six sets ringing Oahu at the time.

Shortly before 7 a.m., Lockard saw a huge formation on the radar's screen. Thinking it was a false reading, he checked the radar set and determined it was operating correctly. At 7:02 a.m., he began tracking a formation of aircraft 132 miles north of Oahu, heading toward the island from three degrees east. Lockard and Elliott should have been at breakfast, but the truck that was supposed to pick them up was late. With nothing to do, they continued to monitor the formation as it approached the island.

Eighteen minutes later, Lockard phoned Fort Shafter to report his findings. Private Joseph McDonald took the call, but with everyone gone to morning chow, he transferred the call to the only officer on duty, Lt. Kermit A. Taylor. After listening to Lockard, and without providing an explanation, Taylor told the young private, "Don't worry about it." What Taylor didn't relay was his knowledge of a flight of twelve B-17 Flying Fortress bombers en route that night from Hamilton Field, north of San Francisco, to Hickam Field, which adjoins Pearl Harbor.

Lockard and Elliott were tracking the first attack wave of 189 Japanese aircraft heading for the military installations on Oahu. It turns out that the planes were launched from a point approximately 260 miles north of Pearl Harbor at 26 degrees north longitude, 158 degrees west latitude.

PREPARING FOR FIRST CALL TO COLORS

The U.S. Navy first adopted the practice of raising the colors at 8 a.m. back in 1843. This tradition was adopted from the British Royal Navy, and the exact time for raising the flag varied by latitude and time of year until it was officially set at 8 a.m. local time in 1870. The tradition is to have the "first call to colors" at 7:55 a.m. to give sailors time to line up on deck for the flag-raising ceremony. Of course, many sailors will gather early to chat and catch up with shipmates before the day officially gets under way.

Sunday, December 7, 1941, was typical for those ships docked in Pearl Harbor. Sunlight shone down on the warships through a deck of broken and scattered clouds that covered the anchorage at 5,000 feet. All throughout the naval station and on board ships, sailors were assembling for the morning's flag-raising ceremony. In the minutes before the yellow and green preparative (or "prep") pennant reached the top of the staff signifying the first call to colors, aircraft engines could be heard in the distance, approaching the harbor.

Minutes earlier, when crossing the Oahu coast, Lt. Cmdr. Mitsuo Fuchida, the flight leader of the Japanese squadrons, signaled to his flight that they had achieved complete surprise. At 7:49 a.m., he gave the order to begin the attack. Approaching Pearl Harbor at 7:53, Fuchida sent the coded message *Tora, Tora, Tora* to the fleet, confirming the attack's surprise as the fighters descended to begin strafing the air field at Ford Island while the torpedo bombers lined up on the battleships and cruisers in the harbor.

From high above the harbor, nine dive-bombers descended, each aiming for the hangars and aircraft parked on the tarmac of Naval Station Pearl Harbor on Ford. U.S. Army Gen. Walter Short, tasked with defending the military installations on Oahu, had alerted all airfields to the possibility of sabotage attacks. Short ordered all aircraft parked in rows, wingtip-to-wingtip, to make the planes easier to guard. The general also ordered that the bullets be removed from each aircraft's machine guns at nightfall. As the Japanese Aichi D3A Val dive-bombers descended, they were presented with an easy target.

Ford Island was home to Patrol Wing 2's PBY Catalinas and also served as the overhaul station for all naval carrier-based aircraft in the region. Thirty-three of the seventy aircraft on Ford were destroyed in the opening seconds of the attack by the flight of Val dive bombers. Their bombs destroyed Hangar 6 and heavily damaged Hangar 38. From his headquarters on Ford, Rear Adm. Patrick N. L. Bellinger sent a message to all naval commands: "Air Raid, Pearl Harbor. This Is No Drill." The message was sent at 7:58 a.m.

The torpedo attack on Battleship Row began at 7:57 a.m. as twelve Nakajima B5N Kate bombers flew into the harbor from the southeast, passing over the fuel tank farm, and heading directly for the ships on the eastern side of Ford Island. Skimming the water at 50 feet, the Kates dropped torpedoes fitted with wooden boxes around the fins to prevent the missiles from diving deep into the harbor and becoming stuck in the mud. Five of the battleships—*Arizona* (BB-39), *California* (BB-44), *Nevada* (BB-36), *Oklahoma* (BB-37), and *West Virginia* (BB-48)—were struck in the first pass. *Oklahoma* took three more torpedoes on the second pass and began a severe list to port. As the Kates passed overhead, gunners in the rear cockpit strafed the ships.

Torpedo-bombers next attacked ships across the channel from Ford Island, sending an underwater missile at the minelayer *Oglala* (CM-4), berthed outside the light cruiser *Helena* (CL-50) along 1010 dock. *Helena* and *Oglala* were berthed at the pier usually reserved for *Pennsylvania* (BB-38), which was in dry dock. A single torpedo passed under *Oglala* and struck *Helena*, flooding one engine and boiler room and shorting the wiring to the main and 5-inch batteries. Generator power was restored to the turrets, which immediately began engaging the low-flying aircraft. Captain R. H. English's crew isolated the flooding and were able to keep the cruiser afloat. The torpedo's concussion, however, split open *Oglala*'s hull plates, and she began to take on water. Minutes later, a bomb was dropped between the two ships, knocking out power to *Oglala*'s pumps. The minelayer was abandoned, but its crew enlisted the aid of a tug, which moved it to the pier behind *Helena*. Two hours after the attack, *Oglala* capsized while tied to 1010 dock.

The first wave's torpedo attacks concluded with Kates skimming low over the Middle Loch near Pearl City to launch against the World War I–era battleship *Utah* (AG-16) that had been modified into a target ship, the light cruisers *Raleigh* (CL-7) and *Detroit* (CL-8), and the seaplane tender *Tangier* (AV-8). Torpedoes missed both *Detroit* and *Tangier*, but the others were not so lucky. *Utah* was moored at F-9, a spot usually reserved for aircraft carriers, and was struck by a pair of torpedoes in rapid succession. By 8:12 a.m., *Utah* had rolled over and sank, taking six officers and fifty-two enlisted men with her. *Detroit*'s crew

fought gallantly to keep their cruiser afloat. A single torpedo flooded the Number Two fire room and the forward engine room. Quickly counter-flooding the listing ship, the crew worked to add additional lines to the mooring floats to keep the ship on an even keel. A Kate from the second wave dropped an armor-piercing bomb directly on *Detroit*, but the heavy bomb penetrated straight through the lightly armored ship to explode on the harbor bottom. Also during the second wave, the unscathed *Tangier*'s guns scored direct hits on three aircraft that were seen to crash.

Simultaneous to the torpedo attacks, high-level bombers were descending on the fleet. Already reeling from the impact of a torpedo hit under its number one turret, *Arizona* was struck by a bomb that set the forward 14-inch magazine on fire. The magazine exploded, destroying the bow section with a force that has been estimated as a one kiloton. The blast killed hundreds of men instantly, including Rear Adm. Isaac C. Kidd, commander of Battleship Division One and the first flag rank officer to die in World War II, as well as the ship's commander, Capt. Franklin Van Valkenburgh. Both were awarded posthumous Medals of Honor.

Arizona was then hit with another bomb near the funnel, followed by a third bomb that exploded on the boat deck, and a fourth hit the number four turret. Four more bombs struck the superstructure amidships. Lt. Cmdr. Samuel G. Fuqua was the surviving senior officer. He directed the damage control efforts and the removal of the wounded from the ships decks. Fuqua also gave the order to abandon ship and was one of the last to leave it. He, too, was awarded the Medal of Honor for his actions. *Arizona* settled upright on the bottom of the harbor, taking 47 officers and 1,056 men with her.

Moored alongside *Arizona*, the repair ship *Vestal* (AR-4) was rocked when the battleship exploded, blowing Cmdr. Cassin Young, the ship's captain, over the side. *Vestal* then took two bomb hits while Young was swimming back to the ship. Once on board, Young moved his ship away from the burning battleship and beached it on Aiea Shoal. For his actions, Young was awarded the Medal of Honor.

Tennessee (BB-43) was moored ahead of *Arizona* and inside *West Virginia*. Oil from the *Arizona* was floating on the surface of the harbor, on fire, and threatened both battleships. Pinned between Ford Island and *West Virginia* with the sky obscured by thick, black smoke, *Tennessee*'s gunners could not see to shoot at any of the attacking planes, and conversely, the Japanese could not see *Tennessee* as a target. While the crew attempted to fight the fire on the water, the rear of the ship was engulfed in flame. High-flying Japanese bombers scored two hits on *Tennessee*, one each on top of Turret Number Two and Turret Number Three. The bombs they dropped were converted 14- or 15-inch armor-piercing shells used on the Japanese fleet's battleships. When the attack was over, *Tennessee* was afloat, but salvage crews had to dynamite the forward mooring quay to untrap the vessel.

West Virginia was mortally wounded in the first torpedo pass by three torpedoes that struck below the ship's armor belt and one that impacted the belt. Two more torpedoes are thought to have entered through the first torpedoes' impact holes—when the ship was listing to port more than 20 degrees and gutting many parts of the battleship's aft interior. The rudder was blown off the ship and was later found on the bottom of the harbor. High-level bombers dropped two 15-inch shells on *West Virginia*, but neither exploded and were later found inside the ship. Fuel oil on fire from *Arizona* entered the ship and added to the conflagration. The fires became so intense that the ship was abandoned, and the crew moved to *Tennessee* to help fight fires there.

Forty minutes after the attack, *Oklahoma* graphically represented the destructive power of naval aviation. Struck by five and possibly as many as seven torpedoes in the opening salvos of the attack, sailors attempted to isolate the flooding, but it was too late. The ship immediately listed to 30 degrees. As more bombs fell, the weight of the water inside the battleship increased. The crew began to abandon ship toward the starboard side as the battleship began to turn. At 8:32 a.m., *Oklahoma*'s list to port became too great and the ship rolled over. A number of men were trapped inside and a rescue effort was begun while the Japanese were still overhead.

Maryland (BB-46) was the most fortunate ship in the harbor that morning. Berthed inside *Oklahoma*, and in the same predicament as *Tennessee,* she was sheltered from torpedo attack as her berth-mate began to roll over. None of the torpedoes launched that morning struck her as *Oklahoma* formed a protective barrier facing the inner harbor. Obscured by smoke from *Arizona, Tennessee,* and *West Virginia*, most of the Japanese pilots ignored *Maryland* and went after more visible prey.

Moored at F-3, directly across from 1010 dock, *California* was preparing for an inspection on Monday, December 8. Six manhole covers into the ship's double bottom had been removed and the nuts of an additional twelve had been loosened. When two

torpedoes struck the ship during the first wave, *California* quickly flooded. Ensign Edgar M. Fain ordered counter-flooding that prevented the battleship from rolling over. A high-level bomber scored a hit amidships, which started a raging fire. As *California* slowly settled lower in the water, the floating fuel oil fire from other damaged battleships began to approach the ship. The fires became so intense that at 10:15, Capt. J. W. Bunkley, *California*'s commanding officer, ordered the ship abandoned. When the fires moved away, the order was rescinded. Three days later, *California* settled to the bottom of the harbor, listing five and one-half degrees to port.

Moored to Berth F-4, the gasoline wharf, tanker *Neosho* (AO-23) had just finished unloading aviation fuel to tanks on Ford when the Japanese appeared overhead. As the fires spread around *California* and threatened the tanker, *Neosho* slipped her lines and backed away from Ford, seeking safer refuge. Moving the tanker also opened an escape route for *Maryland*, but she was pinned to her berth by *Tennessee*.

Tied up at Berth F-8, *Nevada* had steam in its boilers when the attack began. A torpedo hit the ship around 8:10 a.m. as bombers in the rear of the Japanese formation sought undamaged targets. A four- to five-degree list to port was addressed by counter-flooding and making the ship water tight—known as Condition Zed.

Burning fuel oil from *Arizona* began to engulf the water around *Nevada* when the senior officer present, Lt. Cmdr. J. F. Thomas, ordered the ship moved to a safer location. Steaming down the channel past *Arizona* and *Oklahoma* at approximately 9 a.m., five dive-bombers pounced on *Nevada* in an attempt to sink it and block the channel. One bomb hit the ship, passed through the side, and exploded in the harbor; two bombs struck the forecastle; another bomb exploded in the gasoline tank; and the fifth bomb pierced the deck near the Number One turret. Seven minutes later, more bombs rained down on the ship, one striking the port gun director platform, and another demolishing the crew's galley. Realizing that his ship may indeed block the channel if sunk, Thomas ran the battleship into the mud. Tugs arrived and nursed the ship across the channel where she sat with her stern aground and bow afloat.

The second wave of attacks saw fifteen dive-bombers attack ships in the Navy Yard and dry dock area, including the battleship *Pennsylvania* (BB-38) and the destroyers *Cassin* (DD-372) and *Downes* (DD-375). *Pennsylvania* was struck by a bomb that penetrated the main deck, amid ships, causing a fire.

Two officers and sixteen men were killed in the blast. Immediately the dry dock was ordered flooded to within a foot of flotation in case the Japanese burst open the dock. Forward in the dry dock, off the battleship's port bow, sat *Cassin*, with *Downes* off the starboard side. Around 8:50 a.m., ten to fifteen bombers approached the dock area. Destroyer *Shaw* (DD-373) in Floating Drydock Number 2 took a bomb to its forward magazine, which promptly exploded, blowing off the ship's bow. *Cassin* and *Downes* suffered a number of bomb hits that ignited magazines and stored torpedoes, and fires on one ship fed the other. *Cassin* rolled over to starboard, pinning *Downes*.

Seaplane tender *Curtiss* (AV-4) was the victim of a Val's dive-bombing attack. One small bomb detonated on the main deck, taking the lives of twenty-one men and wounding another fifty-eight. Immediately exacting revenge upon the Japanese, *Curtiss*'s gunners scored direct hits on a Val that was pulling out of a dive. Killing the pilot, the plane flew out of control and crashed into *Curtiss*'s forward starboard crane. The Val burned on the deck, destroying some of the ship's wiring, pipes, and steam lines.

Just as the high-altitude bombers completed their mission at 9:15 a.m., twenty-seven Vals returned to strafe the harbor.

AIRCRAFT ALLOCATIONS, OAHU, TERRITORY OF HAWAII, DECEMBER 7, 1941

Hickam Field		Wheeler Field		Bellows Field	
B-17D	12	P-40C	12	O-49	2
B-18	32	P-40B	87	O-47B	7
A-20A	12	P-36A	39	B-18	1
P-26A	2	P-26A	6		
A-12A	2	P-26B	6		
C-33	2	B-12A	3		
B-24A	1	AT-6	4		
		OA-9	3		
		OA-8	1		

ARMY AIR FORCES AIRCRAFT DESTROYED

A-20A	2
B-17C	2
B-17D	6
B-18	11
B-24A	1
P-26A	5
P-26B	1
P-36A	4
P-40B	38
P-40C	4
OA-9	2
O-49	1
Total	77

JAPANESE AIRCRAFT TAIL CODES

Ship	Tail Code
Akagi	AI-
Hiryu	BII-
Kaga	AII-
Soryu	BI-
Shokaku	EI-
Zuikaku	EII-

JAPANESE AIR ATTACK ORDER OF BATTLE

First Attack Aircraft

Unit	Carrier	Type	Armament	Target
First Group—Horizontal Bombers				
1st Attack Unit	Akagi	15 Kates	1 x 800 kg AP	Battleship Row
2nd Attack Unit	Kaga	14 Kates	1 x 800 kg AP	Battleship Row
3rd Attack Unit	Soryu	10 Kates	1 x 800 kg AP	Battleship Row
4th Attack Unit	Hiryu	10 Kates	1 x 800 kg AP	Battleship Row
Torpedo Bombers				
1st Special Attack Unit	Akagi	12 Kates	1 x 800 kg torpedo	Battleships/Carriers
2nd Special Attack Unit	Kaga	12 Kates	1 x 800 kg torpedo	Battleships/Carriers
3rd Special Attack Unit	Soryu	8 Kates	1 x 800 kg torpedo	Battleships/Carriers
4th Special Attack Unit	Hiryu	8 Kates	1 x 800 kg torpedo	Battleships/Carriers
Second Group—Dive Bombers				
15th Attack Unit	Shokaku	27 Vals	1 x 250 kg bomb	Air Bases: Ford Island and Wheeler Field
16th Attack Unit	Zuikaku	27 Vals	1 x 250 kg bomb	Air Bases: Ford Island and Wheeler Field
Third Group—Air Superiority Fighters and Strafers				
1 Fighter Striking Unit	Akagi	9 Zeros	2 x 20mm, 2 x 7.7mm machine guns	Air Superiority, strafing
2 Fighter Striking Unit	Kaga	9 Zeros	2 x 20mm, 2 x 7.7mm machine guns	Air Superiority, strafing
3 Fighter Striking Unit	Soryu	9 Zeros	2 x 20mm, 2 x 7.7mm machine guns	Air Superiority, strafing
4 Fighter Striking Unit	Hiryu	6 Zeros	2 x 20mm, 2 x 7.7mm machine guns	Air Superiority, strafing
5 Fighter Striking Unit	Shokaku	6 Zeros	2 x 20mm, 2 x 7.7mm machine guns	Air Superiority, strafing
6 Fighter Striking Unit	Zuikaku	6 Zeros	2 x 20mm, 2 x 7.7mm machine guns	Air Superiority, strafing

Second Attack Aircraft

Unit	Carrier	Type	Armament	Target
First Group—Horizontal Bombers				
5th Attack Unit	Shokaku	27 Kates	1 x 250 kg bomb, 6 x 60 kg bombs	NAS Kaneohe Bay and NAS Pearl Harbor
6th Attack Unit	Zuikaku	27 Kates	1 x 250 kg bomb, 6 x 60 kg bombs	NAS Kaneohe Bay and NAS Pearl Harbor
Second Group – Dive Bombers				
11th Attack Unit	Soryu	18 Vals	1 x 250 kg bomb	Carriers, Cruisers
12th Attack Unit	Hiryu	27 Vals	1 x 250 kg bomb	Carriers, Cruisers
13th Attack Unit	Akagi	18 Vals	1 x 250 kg bomb	Carriers, Cruisers
14th Attack Unit	Kaga	18 Vals	1 x 250 kg bomb	Carriers, Cruisers
Third Group – Air Superiority Fighters and Strafers				
1st Fighter Strike Unit	Akagi	9 Zeros	*	Hickam Field
2nd Fighter Strike Unit	Kaga	9 Zeros	*	Hickam, Pearl Harbor, Wheeler
3rd Fighter Strike Unit	Soryu	9 Zeros	*	NAS Kaneohe Bay
4th Fighter Strike Unit	Hiryu	9 Zeros	*	Kaneohe Bay, Bellows

Notes: Numbers of aircraft are those planned for the attack. AP = Armor Piercing; Conversions: 60 kg = 132 pounds, 250 kg = 551 pounds; 800 kg = 1,764 pounds; Zero armament: 2 x 20mm cannon and 2 x 7.7mm machine guns.

Source: United States Strategic Bombing Survey (Pacific), *The Campaigns of the Pacific War.*

HICKAM FIELD AND EWA MARINE CORPS AIR STATION

When flying from west to east approaching Pearl Harbor and Hickam Field around the southwestern tip of Oahu lies Ewa Mooring Mast Field. Originally constructed in 1925 as a landing mat for the U.S. Navy's aircraft carrying dirigibles, it was intended that the dirigibles such as *Akron* and *Macon* would scout ahead of the fleet as its ships moved from one point to another. The field was commissioned Marine Corps Air Station Ewa on February 3, 1941.

Ewa Field and the army's Hickam Field on the eastern side of the harbor were rendered impotent within minutes of the Japanese attack. Ewa Field was hit first by six Zeros that approached at 1,000 feet and dived to within 25 feet of the ground to strafe planes and Marines attempting to fight back. Since Ewa was on the way to Pearl Harbor, other Zeros and Vals made a strafing pass at the field either en route to the target, or when returning to the carriers. Marine's broke out machine guns from the armory and were able to position one SBD dive bomber for use as an anti-aircraft gun mount. Ewa Marines are credited with downing one Zero during the battle. By the time the attack had ended at 10 a.m., nearly three quarters of the forty-eight aircraft on the tarmac were ablaze.

Attacks on Hickam Field were well planned and precise. Home to the 18th Bombardment Squadron's long-range four-engine B-17 Flying Fortresses and twin-engine B-18 Bolo bombers, these aircraft were perceived as a large threat to the Japanese fleet. The first attack on the field lasted ten minutes and saw twelve Vals strike the Hawaiian Air Depot. As the machine shops and hangars of the depot exploded, seven more Vals strafed the flight line. At 8:25 a.m., another flight of Vals scored a direct hit on the airfield's fuel pumping system, a number of the technical buildings, and the barracks. A third run on the field was made at 9 a.m., when nine aircraft strafed the hangar line and shop area while an additional half dozen machine-gunned the living quarters, parade ground, and post exchange.

KANEOHE BAY NAVAL AIR STATION AND BELLOWS FIELD

By air, Kaneohe Bay is only fourteen miles to the east, just under three and one-half minutes flying time from Pearl Harbor. As the attack commenced on Pearl Harbor, Zero fighters from *Hiryu* and *Soryu* descended upon the Naval Air Station at Kaneohe Bay and began the attack. Three of the base's aircraft were on patrol when the Japanese arrived overhead. The remaining seaplanes were moored in the bay, parked on the tarmac, and under repair in the base's hangars. The first attack lasted nearly fifteen minutes, just long enough to set half the aircraft ablaze.

When the Zeros departed, squadron personnel went into action, attempting to save the undamaged aircraft and put out those on fire. With the entire base turned out to fight the fires, a flight of *Shokaku* and *Zuikaku* Kates dropped bombs on the air station, scoring a direct hit on Hangar One, destroying the four PBY Catalinas inside. This hangar was burned to its metal structure, but would be salvageable.

Machine guns were rigged in aircraft and on temporary mounts to fire back at the attackers. Side arms and rifles were distributed giving many sailors the opportunity to fire back at the strafing Zeros. When the Japanese left for the last time, only six damaged PBYs remained to greet the three that were out on patrol.

WHEELER FIELD, SCHOFIELD BARRACKS, AND BELLOWS FIELD

At 8:02 a.m., Wheeler Field and the Schofield Barracks, located in the center of the island on Leilehua Plain, came under attack by twenty-five Aichi D3A Val dive-bombers from *Shokaku* and *Zuikaku*, supported by Zeros from *Kaga*. Of the more than 150 Army Air Forces planes at Wheeler Field that morning, nearly eighty were parked wingtip-to-wingtip in rows only twenty feet apart. Diving down from 5,000 feet, the Vals bombed Wheeler Field's hangars and returned for low-level strafing of the ramp and barracks area. The attack lasted fifteen minutes; then the men began the task of fighting fires and attempting to arm planes for combat. At 9 a.m., seven Japanese planes returned for a few quick strafing passes en route back to the carriers. Eighty-three planes were destroyed or heavily damaged at this one airfield alone.

Wheeler Field's auxiliary strip, Bellows Field, located on the eastern side of Oahu and south of Kaneohe Bay, saw only one Zero during the first minutes of the attack. This aircraft strafed the tent area and then flew off. At 9 a.m., nine more Zeros from *Hiryu* turned their attention to Bellows Field destroying three of the twenty aircraft parked there.

Thirty minutes later, at 9:45 a.m., the aerial assault on Pearl Harbor and Oahu's military installations was over. The attackers withdrew from the target area and met over the ocean 20 miles from Kaena Point bearing 340 degrees. Without a large margin of fuel, the Japanese force had to attack, then immediately return to the carriers. Two waves of high-level and torpedo bombers escorted by fighters did tremendous damage during the one hour, forty-five minute attack.

A third wave was not launched since the Japanese believed they had achieved their objective—to destroy the U.S. Pacific Fleet and prevent it from retaliating against Japanese expansion in the eastern Pacific—and since there was the distinct possibility of a retaliatory strike against the Japanese fleet by U.S. land-based bombers and naval patrol aircraft and by the unaccounted-for American aircraft carriers. Under those circumstances, Admiral Nagumo turned his fleet for the home islands.

THE JAPANESE PRESENTATION AND ITS MISSED TARGETS

In Washington, D.C., Japanese delegation members Saburo Kurusu and Admiral Nomura presented their message to Secretary Hull at 2:20 p.m. local time (8:50 a.m. Hawaiian time), nearly an hour after the attack on Pearl Harbor began.

After reading the document, Secretary Hull said to Kurusu and Admiral Nomura, "I must say that in all my conversation with you during the last nine months I never uttered one word of untruth. This is borne out absolutely by the record. In all of my 50 years of public service I have never seen a document that was more crowded with infamous falsehood and distortions—on a scale so huge that I never imagined until today any government on this planet was capable of uttering them."

Whether the message was delivered on time or not, the fact that the Pearl Harbor attack fleet sailed on November 26 showed Japan's clear intention to engage America in war.

None of the Pacific Fleet's carriers were at Pearl Harbor on the morning of December 7. *Saratoga* (CV-3) was more than 2,000 miles away at San Diego, preparing to return to Hawaiian waters. On November 28, *Enterprise* (CV-6) and Task Force 8 (three cruisers, and nine destroyers), under the command of

Adm. William "Bull" Halsey, left Pearl Harbor transporting Marine Fighter Squadron VMF-211 to Wake Atoll. When the attack occurred, the carrier was less than 200 miles from its destination. After refueling and resupplying, *Enterprise* sortied from the harbor on December 8 to patrol against a possible second Japanese attack. On December 10, SBDs from *Enterprise*'s air wing sank *I-70* north of the Hawaiian Islands.

The Pacific Fleet's last carrier, *Lexington* (CV-2), was part of Task Force 12 (three cruisers and five destroyers, under Adm. J. H. Newton) had been dispatched to Midway Island with twenty-five scout bombers for the Marine Corps. At the time of the attack, Task Force 12 was still 460 miles from Midway. Also out at sea during the attack was Adm. Wilson Brown and Task Force 3, centered around the cruiser *Indianapolis* (CA-35), accompanied by five destroyer minesweepers. Task Force 3 was at Johnston Island to test a new type of landing craft. Immediately after the attack, Task Force 3 was recalled and joined Task Force 12, with Admiral Brown assuming command.

On the surface, the Japanese attack on Pearl Harbor looked like a victory—which it was in the short term. However, the attack missed a large number of strategic targets—for example, the submarine base, oil storage tanks, and fuel farm—and left intact many of the shops in the Navy Yard. This infrastructure would enable the U.S. Navy and Army Air Forces to recover more quickly than the Japanese anticipated. In addition, by destroying America's battleships while letting its aircraft carriers remain afloat forced a change of tactics. No longer would battle groups be based around battleships; instead, the navy's task forces would, from then on, center around aircraft carriers.

America lost 2,402 military personnel killed and 1,178 wounded, and 188 hard to replace aircraft were also destroyed in the attack. With eight battleships heavily damaged or sitting on the bottom of the harbor, the Pacific Fleet had to rely on its aircraft carriers to take the battle back to the Japanese.

Japanese Navy Type 99 Carrier Bombers (Val) prepare to take off from an aircraft carrier during the morning of December 7. Ship in the background is the carrier *Soryu*. NARA 80-G-182259

Japanese naval aircraft warm up their engines prior to striking Pearl Harbor. The aircraft carrier (reportedly *Shokaku*) launched twenty-seven dive-bombers and six Zero fighters in the first attack wave of planes on the morning of December 7. Plane in the foreground is an A6M Zero Fighter. NARA 80-G-71198

Akagi Zeros on deck ready to launch for the first-wave attacks. The carrier *Akagi* launched nine Zero fighters in each attack wave. NARA

On the deck of *Akagi*, Zero fighters move into position for launch. NARA

A Japanese Navy Type 97 Kate bomber lifts off from the deck of the carrier *Shokaku*. It is following another Kate, which can be seen at the top of the photo. *Shokaku* sent twenty-seven Kates in the second attack wave. NARA 80-G-182249

A Japanese Navy Zero fighter (tail code A1-108) lifts off from the aircraft carrier *Akagi*, on its way to attack Pearl Harbor during the morning of December 7. 80-G-182252

A Japanese Navy Type 97 Carrier Attack Plane (Kate) takes off from a carrier as the second-wave attack is launched. Ship's crewmen are cheering *banzai*. This ship is either *Zuikaku* or *Shokaku*. Note light tripod mast at the rear of the carrier's island, with Japanese naval ensign. NH50603

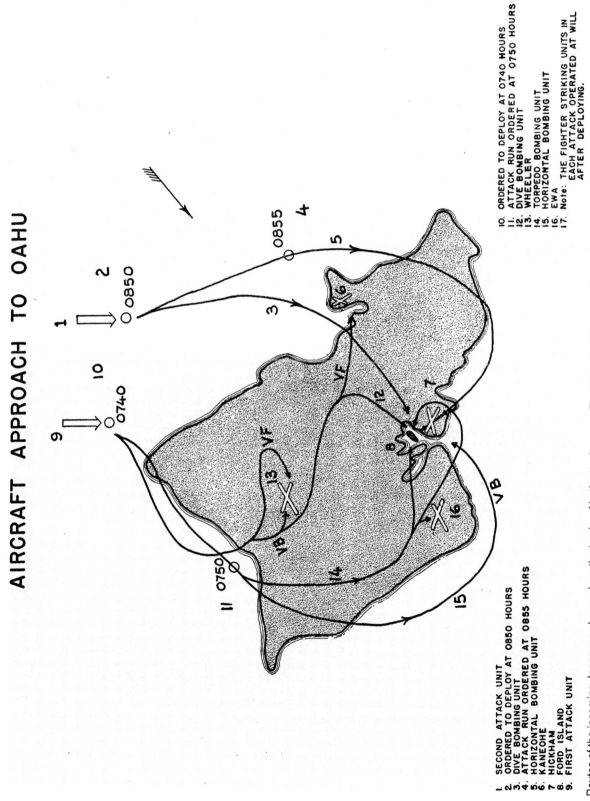

AIRCRAFT APPROACH TO OAHU

1. SECOND ATTACK UNIT
2. ORDERED TO DEPLOY AT 0850 HOURS
3. DIVE BOMBING UNIT
4. ATTACK RUN ORDERED AT 0855 HOURS
5. HORIZONTAL BOMBING UNIT
6. KANEOHE
7. HICKHAM
8. FORD ISLAND
9. FIRST ATTACK UNIT

10. ORDERED TO DEPLOY AT 0740 HOURS
11. ATTACK RUN ORDERED AT 0750 HOURS
12. DIVE BOMBING UNIT
13. WHEELER
14. TORPEDO BOMBING UNIT
15. HORIZONTAL BOMBING UNIT
16. EWA
17. Note: THE FIGHTER STRIKING UNITS IN EACH ATTACK OPERATED AT WILL AFTER DEPLOYING.

Routes of the incoming Japanese planes show the tracks of both attack waves. The first attack destroyed most of the American planes on the ground at Wheeler Field, Naval Air Station Kaneohe Bay, Ewa Mooring Mast Field, Hickam Field, and Naval Air Station Pearl Harbor on Ford Island, achieving air superiority over the island. Bellows Army Air Field and Haleiwa Field were targets of opportunity for the Japanese. The second wave concentrated on inflicting additional damage on the U.S. Pacific Fleet in the harbor. U.S. STRATEGIC BOMBING SURVEY

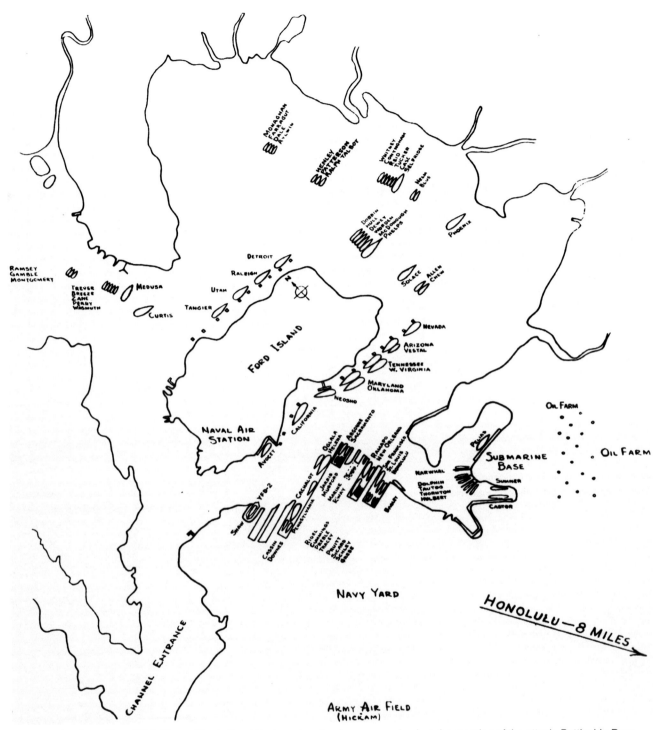

This was the disposition of U.S. Navy ships in Pearl Harbor when the Japanese arrived on the morning of the attack. Battleship Row presented a series of prime targets with an excellent torpedo-launching corridor formed by the channel in front of the Navy Yard's dock area. Most of the ships in the Naval Yard's docks are close together, and it is surprising more damage was not done to this area. Destroyers *Cassin* and *Downes*, battleship *Pennsylvania*, cruiser *Helena*, and minelayer *Oglala* were all situated along 1010 Dock, while destroyer *Shaw* was nearby in floating dry dock *YFD-2*. On the northwest side of Ford Island, seaplane tender *Tangier*, training ship *Utah*, and cruisers *Raleigh* and *Detroit* were exposed in an area wide open for torpedo attacks. The submarine base and fuel farm (center right) were untouched by the Japanese, which many consider a huge strategic mistake on the part of the attackers. NH50931

Captured Japanese photograph showing the opening moments of the attack on Pearl Harbor and surrounding military installations. Hickam Field, the largest counterattack threat to the Japanese attack fleet, burns in the background. All hell is about to break loose on Battleship Row (foreground). Ships on Battleship Row are, from lower left: *Nevada*, repair ship *Vestal* outboard of *Arizona, Tennessee* inboard of *West Virginia, Oklahoma* outboard of *Maryland*, the tanker *Neosho*, and *California*. The torpedo tracks in the harbor point at *Oklahoma*, and it appears that the first underwater missile has begun to explode. Many believe the rooster tails at the torpedo's point of origin show a midget submarine launching torpedoes. Directly above *Oklahoma*, on the far side of the harbor, is the 1,010-foot long—and appropriately named—1010 Dock, where destroyers *Cassin* and *Downes* are already burning. During the following ten minutes after this photo was taken, 2,402 American servicemen lost their lives, 1,178 were wounded, and a world was at war. NH 50931

On the western side of Ford Island, the target ship *Utah* (AG-16) has already taken its first hit while, on Battleship Row, a geyser of water sprouts from *Oklahoma*. A Japanese aircraft can be seen to the right, passing over the Pearl Harbor Naval Yard, having just attacked installations on Hickam Field. 80-G-30554

A Japanese bomber took this photograph looking straight down on Battleship Row as the horizontal bombing attack got underway. Ships visible are (from left to right): *Nevada*; *Arizona* with *Vestal* moored outboard; *Tennessee* with *West Virginia* moored inboard; *Maryland* with *Oklahoma* moored outboard; and tanker *Neosho*, its stern partially visible at the extreme right. Bombs have been dropped on *Arizona* near the stern, but the shell that exploded the battleship's forward magazine has not scored a direct hit yet. Bunker fuel from *West Virginia* and *Oklahoma* is rushing out of their hulls and can be seen on the water's surface. *Oklahoma* is beginning to capsize, its port rail already under water. NH 50472

Another view of Battleship Row taken as a bomb hits the *Arizona*, while the battleship *Nevada* appears to be undamaged at this point in the attack. *Oklahoma*, center right, has rolled over and a number of small boats can be seen tracking through the ship's oil slick. Many of these boats pulled oil-covered sailors from the harbor. NH 50932

Japanese strike photo showing the western side of Ford Island with *Utah* already capsized. The cruiser *Raleigh*, to *Utah*'s left, has been severely damaged in the torpedo attack and is starting to list to port. NH 50933

Japanese Zero fighter trails smoke having been hit by anti-aircraft fire. 80-G-19931

A Val dive-bomber drops a 250-kilogram (551-pound) bomb on ships in the harbor. 80-G-32460

A Japanese plane, most likely a Zero fighter, passes over the U.S. submarine *Narwhal* (SS-167) at the harbor's submarine base and heads toward the Pearl Harbor Naval Yard. Smoke to the right is coming from destroyers *Cassin, Downes*, and *Shaw*. 80-G-33053

A Japanese pilot presents the business end of a Val dive-bomber toward an American target. Notice that the aircraft's dive breaks are extended and that the bomb has left its shackle and is on its way to the target. 80-G-32908

Zuikaku launched twenty-seven Kate high-level bombers, each armed with one 250-kilogram bomb or six 60-kilogram bombs. Their targets were NAS Kaneohe and NAS Pearl Harbor. Here *Zuikaku*'s aircraft 307 is seen leaving its target of NAS Pearl Harbor with Battleship Row ablaze. NARA

Telegram received on board the carrier *Wasp* (CV-7) broadcasting the message: "Air raid on Pearl Harbor. This is not drill." At the time of the telegram, *Wasp* was in the Atlantic Ocean. *Wasp* was sunk by the Japanese submarine *I-19* near Guadalcanal on September 15, 1942. NARA

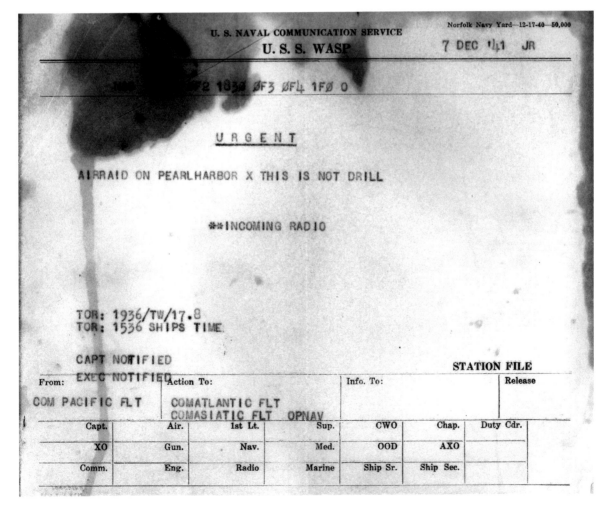

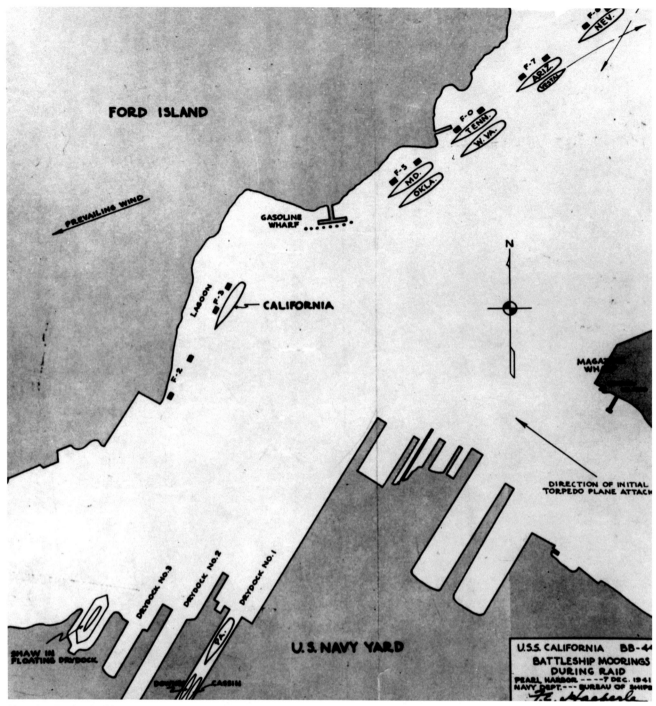

Map showing battleship mooring positions during the Japanese attack. The tanker *Neosho* has moved from its berth at the gasoline wharf, while the map indicated the direction of travel for the repair ship *Vestal* and the battleship *Nevada*. NH 83108

Oklahoma

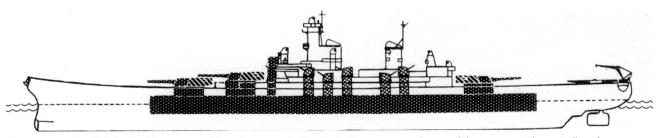

Diagram showing U.S. battleship armor and how the armor belt protects the gun magazines and the spaces at the waterline. As built, the *Oklahoma* had an armor belt that ranged from 8 to 13½ inches thick. The Japanese used their Type 91 aerial torpedo fitted with wooden stabilizers on the fins to prevent the torpedo from diving deep into the harbor's muddy bottom. Each torpedo's warhead contained approximately 450 pounds of high explosives. Battleship *Oklahoma* was struck by three torpedoes, which opened up her bow underwater, and as she started to capsize, two additional torpedoes stuck unarmored parts of the ship. *Oklahoma* was hit by nine torpedoes. U.S. NAVY

Looking north toward Battleship Row, *California* is to the left starting to list to port, and in the distance smoke from the burning *Tennessee* and *Arizona* fills the sky. *Oklahoma*, capsized to port, can be seen with its starboard hull and bottom out of the water. The only thing stopping its roll is the battleship's masts hitting muddy bottom. 80-G-32640

Looking across the harbor from 1010 Dock gives a closer view of *Oklahoma* capsized alongside *Maryland*, with *West Virginia* and *Tennessee* sitting on the bottom. *Arizona* burns in the background, its mast visible to the right of the smoke column. 80-G-32691

Side view of *Oklahoma* and *Maryland* to the left, with *West Virginia* and *Tennessee* burning at right. Sailors on board *Maryland* are attempting to use fire hoses to keep pools of floating, burning oil from reaching the battleship. *Oklahoma* absorbed the brunt of Japanese aerial torpedoes, thereby protecting *Maryland* from damage under the water line. 80-G-33035

Motor boats from *Oklahoma* (foreground) and *Argonne*, next to the upturned hull of *Oklahoma*, cruise the harbor looking to retrieve survivors from the water. Rescue crews can be seen on *Oklahoma*'s hull. On top of *Maryland*'s Turret Number Three, right center of the photo, can be seen the float for the ship's OS2U-3 Kingfisher scout plane, Bureau No. 5288. 80-G-19941

Tennessee burns behind *Maryland* as she sits alongside capsized *Oklahoma*. Men have begun the task of listening for survivors inside *Oklahoma*'s hull. A number of men survived the capsizing, and thirty-two were rescued by workers from the Naval Yard. In total, 429 officers and men were killed in the *Oklahoma*'s capsizing and sinking. *Maryland* suffered a pair of bomb hits and was quickly repaired. She was the first of Pearl Harbor's damaged ships to return to the fleet. NH 83065

West Virginia and *Tennessee*

At Battleship Row's Berth F-6, *Tennessee* was moored inboard of *West Virginia*. Both ships suffered greatly in the first wave of attacks. *West Virginia* absorbed the torpedoes sent toward Berth F-6 and was on the bottom in a matter of minutes. Two bombs struck *Tennessee*, both dropped by high-altitude horizontal bombers. One bomb pierced the roof of Turret Two, but ignited a fire rather than exploding and burned the inside of the turret, causing heavy damage. Splinters from the bomb's impact sprayed the *West Virginia*, killing the ship's commanding officer, Capt. Mervyn S. Bennion, who was awarded the Medal of Honor for his actions that day. The second bomb came through the roof of Turret Three, and it also failed to explode. It burned out the port side interior of the turret. NH 97398

West Virginia burns at the height of the air raid. Her decks are awash and burning bunker oil coats the surface of the harbor fanning the flames on board the battleship.
80-G-19930

Garbage lighter *YG-17* has two hoses spraying water onto the fires on board *West Virginia* while a motor launch pumps water as well. A whale boat from one of the battleships stands by at left. 80-G-19947

Once the fires were extinguished, external damage to *West Virginia* could be seen. Note the gun tubs at left; the deck underneath the guns has been blown out from multiple torpedo hits and is beginning to fall. Both OS2U Kingfishers are completely destroyed as well. The 5-inch/25-caliber gun sits in the stowed position with its canvas sea cover still mounted showing that not all guns were able to engage the attacking Japanese planes. 80-G-19945

Arizona

A sailor aboard the hospital ship *Solace* (AH-5), docked across the harbor to the northwest of *Arizona*, used his movie camera with rare color film to capture the instant the battleship's forward magazine exploded. The explosion was estimated to have the force of one million pounds of dynamite. At the extreme right of the photo, near the leading edge of the fireball, the *Oklahoma*'s mast can be seen rotating through 45 degrees as the battleship capsizes. 80-G-6683

Japanese Kate horizontal bombers scored a direct hit on *Arizona* with a 16-inch battleship shell that had been converted into a 1,760-pound bomb. The bomb penetrated through decks into the forward 14-inch magazine and exploded. The massive blast blew out the sides of the battleship and destroyed the bow of the ship. With a number of decks vaporized, the forward mast collapsed toward the bow. Sailors on board *Tennessee*, at left, are using fire hoses to keep burning oil on the water's surface from engulfing the battleship's stern.
80-G-19942

Arizona continues to burn in the hours after the attack. The damage done to the battleship by the Japanese bombs coupled with the massive explosion of the forward magazine was complete. One bomb struck Turret Four, ricocheting off and then exploding below deck; a second struck the port side amidships, followed by another near the port aft 5-inch anti-aircraft gun. The final 1,760-pound bomb exploded in the forward 14-inch magazine. 80-G-32427

The tug *Hoga* (YT-146) sprays water onto the burning hulk of the *Arizona*. The battleship's aft mast, boat cranes, and searchlight deck appear undamaged. The barrels of *Arizona*'s 14-inch guns in Turret Two can be seen protruding above the waterline at left. 80-G-32485

Stars and stripes forever: The American flag waves in the breeze as the battleship *Arizona* sits on the bottom of Pearl Harbor, its midships section ablaze. Turrets Three and Four would later be salvaged to provide coastal defense guns for Oahu. 80-G-32591

Nevada

While *Nevada* sorties for the harbor entrance, *Avocet*'s gunners are scanning the sky for the next attackers. *Avocet*'s gunners downed the torpedo-bomber that scored a hit on *California*. *Nevada* had two boilers lit when the attack occurred. After the attack was under way, around 8:10 a.m., a Japanese torpedo struck the battleship's port side torpedo blister, causing interior plates to buckle and flooding to begin. The ship began to list, which was brought under control by counter-flooding. At 8:55, the battleship got underway, and as she headed for the mouth of the harbor, Japanese dive-bombers were drawn to her in the hopes of sinking her in the entrance channel. *Nevada* quickly received five bomb hits as she moved past Battleship Row. Several near-missed opened up more hull plates, and at 9:40 a.m., she was beached at Hospital Point. Smoke from the fires on board *Shaw* can be seen at left. 80-G-32445

Beached on Waipio Peninsula Hospital Point, *Nevada* is assisted by the tug *Hoga* as crews attempt to extinguish fires on the battleship's bow. *Nevada* had escaped Battleship Row and was beached at Hospital Point to prevent her from blocking the harbor's entrance channel. To the right of *Nevada*'s lowered boarding ladder are a life boat and the channel marker buoy signifying the shallows of Hospital Point. 80-G-19940

Utah

Moored at Berth F-11 on the west side of Ford Island, *Utah* was struck by a pair of torpedoes in the opening moments of the Japanese attack. Her stern settled on the harbor bottom and the former battleship began to list to port, rolling over by 8:12 a.m. This photograph was taken from the cruiser *Raleigh*, also struck by a torpedo in the same attack. 80-G-266626

Shaw

NH 86118

NH 97417

Two views of the destroyer *Shaw*'s forward magazine exploding as she sat in *YFD-2*, a floating dry dock. The destroyer was targeted by dive-bombers, and the explosion occurred during the second wave of the attack. *Nevada* can be seen moving down the channel on the right side of the photos.

Shaw is seen burning in *YFD-2*, its bow section ablaze. *Nevada* can be seen at right, its bow also on fire. In the dry dock with *Shaw* is the tug *Sotoyomo* (YT-9). Although both ships were heavily damaged, they eventually returned to the fleet. 80-G-32719

After the explosion of *Shaw*'s forward magazines, the blast ruptured plates in the floating dry dock, causing the port side to sink to the harbor bottom. *Shaw* and *Sotoyomo* became buoyant once they were level with the sea. *Sotoyomo* and its single tall smoke stack can be seen just forward of *Shaw* in this image. 80-G-32739

California

Moored at Berth F-3, *California* sounded general quarters at 7:50 a.m. as the Japanese planes approached. Within the next ninety seconds she was struck by a torpedo from a *Kaga* Nakajima Type 97 Kate torpedo-bomber. The battleship has taken on a substantial list. In the background to the right is the tanker *Neosho* (AO-23) that had just transferred a full load of aviation gasoline to Ford Island. *Neosho*'s commanding officer, Cmdr. John S. Phillips, got the tanker underway and moved to a more secluded area of the harbor during the second wave. *Oklahoma*'s overturned hull can be seen to the right of *Neosho*. NARA

View of *California* from Ford Island as the battleship takes on more water and the list increases. 80-G-32463

California seen from one of the many small boats working to rescue sailors in tho harbor shows her port deck awash as she settles to the harbor bottom. Note the OS2U Kingfisher sitting on the catapult above Turret Number Three. *Nevada* can be seen beached at Hospital Point in the center background. 80-G-32456

Minesweeper *Avocet* (AVP-4) was berthed at F-1A, south of Battleship Row. When *California* was attacked, *Avocet*'s gunners downed the Kate torpedo-bomber that scored a hit on the battleship. 80-G-32669

Cassin, *Downes*, and *Pennsylvania*

Looking down the channel alongside 1010 Dock, battleship *Pennsylvania* can be seen in the distance in Dry Dock Number One. The pillar of smoke comes from destroyers *Cassin* and *Downes*, which are burning away. In the center, the minelayer *Oglala* is just visible above the surface, having capsized at the dock. 80-G-32953

The front half of Dry Dock Number One was a complete mess. *Downes* (DD-375), at left, and *Cassin* (DD-372), at right, appear to be total losses. However, *Pennsylvania*, situated behind the destroyers in the dry dock was virtually untouched. The battleship had all three of its propeller shafts removed for overhaul at the time of the attack and was the first of the Pearl Harbor attack victims returned to the fleet. 80-G-32511

Dolphin (SS-169, left) and *Narwhal* (SS-167) tied up alongside Pier Four (*Dolphin* at Berth S-7 and *Narwhal* at S-8) at the Submarine Base. At 7:53 a.m., *Narwhal* sounded the air-raid alarm and went to battle stations. Sailors on board both submarines engaged the Japanese planes with 50-cal and 30-cal machine guns. There were no casualties or damage to the submarine base, and two submarines and a destroyer shared credit for downing one of the attacking planes. *Cachalot* (SS-170) and *Tautog* (SS-199) were also tied up at the submarine base during the attack. NARA

Oglala

Scene of the conflagration inside the Pearl Harbor Navy Yard, with the minelayer *Oglala* capsized and the light cruiser *Helena* (CL-50) to the left. Both ships were moored together, with *Helena* tied to 1010 Dock and *Oglala* outboard. During the first three to five minutes of the attack, a Japanese aerial torpedo was fired at the pair of ships, running under the minelayer and striking the cruiser. When the torpedo detonated, it killed twenty men on the cruiser, which began to flood. Damage control limited the cruiser's list to five degrees, but *Oglala* was mortally wounded. The concussion of the torpedo explosion crushed *Oglala*'s bilge on the port side. Due to turn-of-the-century construction, she was not built to the watertight integrity standards needed by combat vessels of the 1930s. Unable to control the in-rushing water, *Oglala* quickly flooded and capsized. Three distinct columns of smoke can be seen in the background: at left, *Cassin* and *Downes* burn in Dry Dock Number One; at center is *Shaw* in *YFD-2*; and at right, the *Nevada*'s bow burns brightly. 80-G-474789

Sailors stand on the overturned hull of *Oglala* alongside 1010 Dock checking to see if anyone is trapped within. Looking over the sunk *Oglala* to the capsized *Oklahoma* (background), rescue workers can be seen on the battleship's hull beginning the search for survivors. NARA

Curtiss and Vestal

Seaplane tender *Curtiss* (AV-4, left) was moored near the fleet repair ship *Medusa* (AR-1) in the harbor's Middle Loch, north and east of Ford Island. *Curtiss* presented a big target, sitting in the center of the western channel. Lookouts on *Curtiss* spotted a submarine conning tower at 8:35 a.m. Five minutes later, when the midget sub surfaced and fired a torpedo at a nest of destroyers behind the seaplane tender, gunners on board *Curtiss* began firing at the submarine, claiming two hits. At 8:43, destroyer *Monaghan* dropped a pair of depth charges, killing the submarine. 80-G-32733

Three dive-bombers set *Curtiss* in their sights, but only two left the area. One was damaged by anti-aircraft fire and crashed into the ship's Number One crane, and its fuel tank exploded on the deck. The subsequent fire damaged the hangar deck, and one bomb penetrated to explode below decks causing damage to the aircraft repair shops. NH 96660

When the attack began, the fleet repair ship *Vestal* (AR-4) was tied up to *Arizona*. At 7:55 a.m., the ship's gunners started firing back at the attacking planes. Being in the proximity of a capital ship did not bode well for the thirty-three year-old ship. Two bombs struck *Vestal*, one on each side of the ship. The port side bomb went down three decks, exploding and igniting the contents of the stores hold. Situated next to the forward magazine, the magazine was quickly flooded to prevent heat from the stores hold fire from cooking off its contents. The second bomb passed through the shop areas on the starboard side of the ship and exited out the bottom of the hull. When *Arizona's* forward magazine exploded, concussion from the blast blew everyone off the decks of *Vestal*, including the ship's captain, Cmdr. Cassin Young, and started fires on deck. After swimming back to the ship he ordered it off *Arizona*. At 9:10 a.m., *Vestal* was anchored in the northeast section of the harbor, 900 yards off McGrew's Point, but it was quickly evident that the ship was taking on water faster than the holes could be plugged and she was beached at Aiea. 80-G-19933

Death of a Midget Sub

Moments after the attack began, destroyer *Monaghan* (DD-354) was ordered out of the harbor to assist *Ward*. Steaming through East Loch toward the harbor mouth, seaplane tenders *Curtiss* (AV-4) and *Tangier* (AV-8) both spotted a midget submarine and engaged it at 8:37 a.m. *Monaghan* turned to ram the sub, which fired a torpedo at the destroyer. The torpedo passed down *Monaghan*'s starboard side and exploded harmlessly on the shore near the end of its run. *Monaghan* increased speed to ram the submarine and rolled a pair of depth charges as it passed over its last known location. The sub was not heard from again. NARA

The midget sub sunk by *Monaghan* was launched from the Japanese fleet submarine *I-22* on the evening of December 6, about ten miles off the coast of Pearl Harbor. The midget sub, known as *I-22tou*, was able to sneak through the anti-submarine net at the mouth of the harbor and glide undetected into the East Loch area. The concussion of *Monaghan*'s depth charges in the shallow harbor mangled the aft end of the submarine, and it appears that one of the destroyer's depth bombs landed on the bow of the midget and detonated its remaining torpedo as the forward compartment is nearly blown off. NH 54302

In the weeks after the battle, *I-22tou* was recovered from the mud bottom of Pearl Harbor. Heavily damaged by *Monaghan*'s depth charging, the sub was of little intelligence value and was used as fill to expand the dock area near the submarine base. Shortly after this photo was taken, *I-22tou* was rolled into the pit and covered over. The crew of *I-22tou*, Cmdr. Naoji Iwasa and Sub Lt. Naokichi Sasaki, are thought to be entombed in the midget submarine's wreck. Ensign Kazuo Sakamaki's *I-24tou* can be seen disassembled in the background near the railroad crossing sign. NARA

This chart was recovered from a Japanese midget submarine and shows steering tracks around Ford Island and the location of ships in the harbor. This map most likely came from Ensign Kazuo Sakamaki's *I-24tou*, which was captured intact on the beach at Bellows Field after having compass problems and becoming unable to find the harbor entrance. 80-G-413507

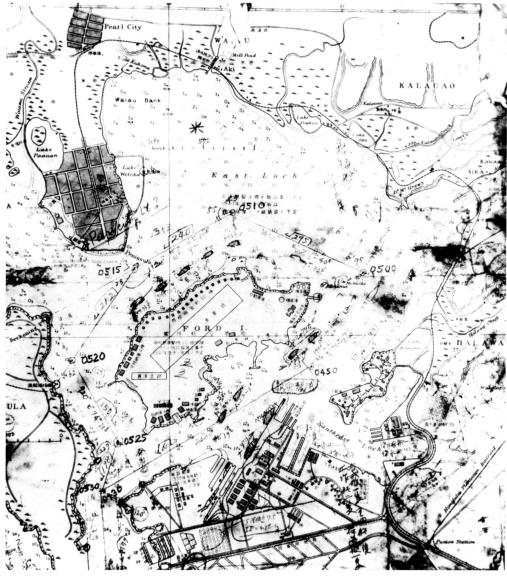

At the height of the battle, anti-aircraft bursts filled the skies over Pearl Harbor. The large black plume of smoke in the foreground of the photo is rising from the mortally wounded *Arizona*. To the left destroyers *Shaw, Cassin*, and *Downes* burn in their docks at the Pearl Harbor Naval Yard.

80-G-40056

Looking toward the Pearl Harbor Navy Yard, Japanese planes continue to bomb and strafe ships in the harbor and the airfield facilities on Ford Island. The black cloud of smoke is from the burning *Arizona*.

NARA

Looking southwest from the Aiea Heights area shortly after the conclusion of the Japanese attack, the entire length of Battleship Row is ablaze while the Navy Yard, to the left, and the ships in dry dock burn. NH 97376

By mid-day on December 8, fires on board *Shaw, Cassin*, and *Downes* have been extinguished, while *Arizona* continues to burn. Fires on the battleship were fought for two and a half days before they were extinguished. NARA

B-17S ARRIVE AT THE HEIGHT OF THE JAPANESE ATTACK

War clouds were approaching in the Far East as fall embraced the United States. To bolster its forces in the Philippines, the War Department decided to send sixteen Flying Fortresses to help protect the island nation and provide an increased offensive capability. Half of the bombers would come from the 38th Reconnaissance Squadron and the remainder from the 88th Reconnaissance Squadron.

All of the aircraft assembled at Hamilton Field, north of San Francisco to be prepared for the long, over-water flight and await favorable weather. In preparation for the flight, long-range fuel tanks were installed in the bomb bays, the bombers' guns were stowed, and no ammunition was to be carried on the flight to Hawaii.

Sixteen aircraft took off from Hamilton Field on December 6 at ten-minute intervals, and for various reasons—mostly engine issues—two bombers from each squadron turned back. Thus, twelve B-17s, four B-17Cs and two B-17Es from the 38th Reconnaissance Squadron and six B-17Es from the 88th Reconnaissance Squadron, continued to Hawaii. The bombers navigated their own way to Hawaii rather than flying in formation, which consumes more fuel as the bombers try to hold position on each other's wing. Once in range of the islands, the Flying Fortresses were able to hone in on the signal from Honolulu radio station KGMB, which was playing music all night to aid the bomber crews in their navigation.

Staff Sgt. Lee Embree took this photo from a 38th Reconnaissance Squadron B-17 as swarms of Japanese dive bombers passed the Flying Fortresses approaching the Pearl Harbor area. The B-17 Embree was flying in landed safely and after the attack the crew removed everything they thought could burn if the bomber was strafed again. SIGNAL CORPS 127014

Nine of the twelve Flying Fortresses coming from California landed at Hickam Field during the attack. One of the B-17s is seen flying away from Hickam over the bow of the minesweeper *Avocet* (AVP-4). A couple of the B-17s had to make more than one approach to Hickam Field. *Avocet* was berthed alongside Ford Island at the south end of Battleship Row, past *California*. NARA 80-G-32458

Bombers from the 38th Reconnaissance Squadron started arriving during the opening moments of the air raid, quickly followed by those from the 88th. Nine of the twelve bombers were able to fly through anti-aircraft fire while being pursued by Japanese fighters to land at Hickam Field. One of the 38th Reconnaissance Squadron's bombers, B-17C 40-2049 *Skipper* was unable to make Hickam and landed at Bellows Field. It was damaged in the attack and was salvaged. From the 88th Reconnaissance Squadron, B-17E 41-2413, flown by 1st Lt. Frank P. Bostrom, was chased away from Hickam Field. Low on gas, Bostrom set down on the Kahuku Golf Course near the northern tip of Oahu. The aircraft was patched up and flown to Hickam Field a few days later.

Flying B-17E 41-2429 *Why Don't We Do This More Often* was the commanding officer of the 88th Reconnaissance Squadron, Capt. Richard Carmichael. Greeted by moderate anti-aircraft fire, Carmichael could see ships burning in Pearl Harbor and an aircraft melee as Japanese planes dive bombed the targets in the area. Deciding not to try for Hickam Field, Carmichael turned for the army's Bellows Field on the eastern side of the island. Arriving while the airstrip was under attack, *Why Don't We Do This More Often* was flown north to land at Haleiwa Field. Once on the ground, Carmichael's B-17 joined that of Lt. Harold N. Chaffin, who had put B-17E 41-2430 *Naughty But Nice* on the field a few minutes earlier.

The radio room fire is evident in this close-up view of B-17C 40-2074, flown by Capt. Raymond T. Swenson. The way the fuselage split saved the main landing gear, engines, and propellers so they could be used to repair other Flying Fortresses damaged in the air raid. NARA 80-G-32915

This photo has been attributed to Staff Sgt. Lee Embree, who turned his camera toward the burning battleship *Arizona*. In the distance is one of the Hawaiian Air Force's B-17Ds wearing the red and white tail stripes seen on many Army Air Forces aircraft of what has now become known as the "prewar" period. U.S. ARMY AIR FORCE

Sitting on Hickam Field were twelve B-17Ds belonging to the Hawaiian Air Force's 5th and 11th Bomb Groups. Parked close to other B-17s and B-18s, the large, four-engine bombers were easy targets for strafing Japanese planes. The Fifth Bomb Group lost two Flying Fortresses (40-3071 and -3080) while the 11th Bomb Group suffered the destruction of two thirds of its bomber force (40-3060, -3077, -3081, and -3083).

After the attack, two B-17s were bombed up and ordered to search for the Japanese fleet. Maj. Truman H. Landon, commanding officer of the 38th Reconnaissance Squadron, who had flown B-17E 41-2413 from California, reported encountering Japanese planes leaving the Pearl Harbor area, flying to the north. In spite of Landon's report, the two B-17s dispatched to find the Japanese, flown by Capt. Brooke E. Allen and Maj. LaVerne Saunders, were ordered to search south of Oahu.

Allen did find a carrier; however, it was the *Enterprise* returning from transferring Marine Fighter Squadron 211 (VMF-211) to Wake Atoll, which is due east and south of Pearl Harbor by 2,340 miles. Although Wake is separated from Hawaii by the International Date Line, it was only a matter of hours after the Pearl Harbor attack that bombs rained down on the airfield there.

Capt. Raymond T. Swenson's B-17C 40-2074 sits broken on the Hickam Field runway. A pair of strafing Japanese fighters hit the flare box in the radio room and started the aircraft burning and wounding Flight Surgeon 1st Lt. William R. Schick, who was a passenger in the bomber. Swenson set the bomber down, which broke in half at the point of the radio room fire. As the crew was evacuating, Zero fighters strafed the aircraft again, wounding bombardier G. C. Beale and navigator 2nd Lt. H. R Taylor. One of the Zero's bullets struck Schick in the head, and he subsequently died from his wounds. U.S. ARMY AIR FORCE

Maintenance crews began repairing B-18s on Hickam Field as soon as the smoke cleared. The B-18 in the background was most likely undergoing an overhaul when the attack occurred as its engines and nose turret have been removed. The B-17 to the left is one of six B-17Ds that were destroyed on the ground during the attack. Its engines and propellers have been pulled to provide spares for other Flying Fortresses that were salvageable. U.S. ARMY AIR FORCE

First Lt. Robert H. Richards tried to land the 38th Reconnaissance Squadron B-17C 40-2049 *Skipper* at Hickam Field, but was pursued by Japanese fighters. He aborted his landing and left the area for safer skies. Running low on fuel, Richards set *Skipper* down on the short airstrip at Bellows Field overrunning the end of the runway. The war for 40-2049 ended here as the bomber was salvaged for parts to repair other B-17s damaged in the attack. U.S. ARMY AIR FORCE

Hickam Field

Three bombs were dropped near the base flag pole, ripping Old Glory, but not destroying her. This flag remained in place during the attack and was subsequently rescued while the building behind was consumed by fire in the hours after the attack. This flag, from America's first battle of World War II, was flown over the United Nations meeting in San Francisco and over the White House when the Japanese surrendered. It is now on display at Hickam Field. NARA

Hickam Field was home to the Hawaiian Air Depot, where Army Air Forces aircraft in the islands underwent heavy maintenance. Many of the aircraft at Hickam were destroyed in strafing attacks, including this pair of P-40s. Note the bullet holes in the hangar windows. NARA

Burned out Curtiss P-40 on the tarmac with the tail of a Boeing P-26 pursuit aircraft visible at right. The P-26 was the Army Air Corps's first all-metal fighter to enter squadron service. P-26s were delivered between 1933 and 1936 and were outclassed by the Mitsubishi A6M the day the war started. NARA

Bombed out hangars and destroyed aircraft litter the Hickam ramp. The seaplane in the foreground appears to be a Navy Vought OS2U Kingfisher. NARA

View from the enlisted men's barracks, toward the Hickam Field flight line between Wing E, left, and Wing D. The front half of a B-17, broken at the radio room, rests on the trailing edge of its wings. NARA

With war clouds on the horizon, the army and navy needed aerial reconnaissance of the Japanese Mandate Islands in the Pacific. It was decided to transfer a pair of B-24As to the 88th Reconnaissance Squadron and fly them from San Francisco to the Philippines via Oahu, Midway Atoll, Wake Island, Port Moresby, New Guinea, then on to Clark Field outside of Manila. En route, they would survey the Japanese strongholds at Jaluit in the Marshall Islands and Truk in the Caroline Islands. The pair of B-24As were dispatched to McClellan Field, outside Sacramento, California, for modifications, then on to Hickam. Both aircraft departed on December 5, 1941, but one turned back. Only B-24A, serial number 40-2371, flown by First Lt. Ted S. Faulkner, completed the flight to Hickam. On the morning of the attack, 40-2371 was parked in front of Hangar 15, and it was destroyed in the attack. Two men were killed, 2nd Lt. Louis G. Moslener Jr. and Pvt. Daniel J. Powlowki, and three were wounded. NARA

The hulk of a bombed-out Douglas B-18 Bolo twin-engine bomber sits in front of Hickam Field's burning hangar row. Both the Fifth and Eleventh Bomb Groups lost B-18s in the attack. NARA

The shop and motorpool areas were also strafed, destroying vehicles and aircraft maintenance facilities. NARA

B-18 bomber engine nacelles were dragged over to a hastily prepared dirt mound to serve as an anti-aircraft machine gun emplacement. The engines and propellers were transported from one of the wrecks on the field, and a heavy shop table was added to protect the defenders. NARA

Hickam Field's Hangar 11 was heavily damaged as was this B-18 outside. Notice the "prewar" red and white tail stripes on what's left of the rudder. NARA

A bomb explosion on the ramp broke a water main under the pavement between Hangars Seven and Eleven. NARA

A bomb crater at Hickam was deep enough for a man to stand in. Note that nearly all of the windows have been blown out of the hangar in the background. NARA

Fifth Bomb Group B-18 Bolos undergoing overhaul at the Hawaiian Air Depot were damaged inside their hangar. The aircraft in the foreground looks restorable, but the Bolo to the left appears to have suffered greater damage. NARA

Hangar and shop building at the Hawaiian Air Depot were heavily damaged in the attack. NARA

The Douglas A-20 Havocs of the 58th Bombardment Group (Light) were in various states of readiness when the attack occurred. Here an A-20 and a North American Aviation O-49 sit in one of the shop hangars at the Hawaiian Air Depot. Fire has consumed the fabric covering from the control surfaces of the aircraft, while the A-20 appears it was undergoing major structural overhaul with the bomber's belly skin open. NARA

Smoke from fires on the flight line hangs over Hickam Field in the hours after the attack. NARA

The barracks adjacent to the parade ground were burning nearly two hours after the attack. Bombs cut many of the water mains on Hickam Field and what few firefighting resources the base had were working to save the Hawaiian Air Depot's shops. NARA

Burned-out truck near Hickam Field parade ground at "F" Street. The truck was still burning more than an hour after the attack had ended. NARA

59989 A.C
127013

Two views of Hickam Field's Hangar Avenue and the damage done to the hangars. Note the bullet holes in the concrete structure made by strafing Japanese planes. NARA

The marauding Japanese fighters strafed everything, including the latrine on Hickam Field. The destroyed restroom was located on Coronet Avenue. NARA

Wrecked truck at Hickam Field. Both the truck and the building behind it suffered from a bomb blast and subsequent strafing. Notice the bullet holes in the cab of the truck. NARA

Blast damage is evident at the post exchange on base. NARA

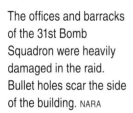

The enlisted men's beer garden earned the name the "Snake Ranch." It had burned down in 1940 and reopened a few months before the December 7 attack. It was completely destroyed in the air raid. NARA

The offices and barracks of the 31st Bomb Squadron were heavily damaged in the raid. Bullet holes scar the side of the building. NARA

Naval Air Station Pearl Harbor

The apron at Pearl Harbor was a mess with sailors trying to save lightly damaged aircraft while extinguishing fires of those burning during the attack. A bulldozer can be seen moving dirt to fill in bomb craters while float-mounted Curtiss SOC Seagulls are moved away from the hangars. NARA

High angle view of the damage caused to the hangars and aircraft on the ramp at NAS Pearl Harbor on Ford Island. A number of aircraft burn on the ramp, including a PBY Catalina at left, and an SBD Dauntless in front of the hangar. Notice the pure flying boat PBY-3 at right. NARA

Wreckage of a burned-out PBY Catalina sits in front of the seaplane hangar on Ford Island. NARA

A destroyed OS2U Kingfisher sits at right while a mechanic services another of the type at left. Sailors on top of the hangar are inspecting bomb damage from the attack. NARA

In the aftermath of the attack, the navy's patrol squadrons gathered the remaining serviceable aircraft to scout for the Japanese fleet. Battleship *Nevada* sits aground on Waipio Peninsula above the hangars. NARA

Naval Air Station Kaneohe Bay

During the second attack wave, Kate high-level bombers from *Shokaku* and *Zuikaku* were sent to drop bombs on the Naval Air Stations at Kaneohe Bay and Pearl Harbor. Their primary targets were the air stations' hangars. NARA

Sailors heave on a line from shore to a burning PBY Catalina floating in Kaneohe Bay after the Japanese attack. The port wing has burned off, and the fabric covered sections of the wing have also been consumed by fire. NH 97432

Naval Air Station Kaneohe Bay was home to three patrol squadrons: VP-11, VP-12, and VP-14. Here the hull of a burned-out VP-12 Catalina sits in a pile of burned PBYs. Three VP-14 PBYs were on patrol that morning and escaped destruction. NARA

Bellows Army Air Field

Japanese fighters set this gasoline truck on fire. The truck was a total loss. NARA

Bellows Field was essentially a target of opportunity for Japanese fighters, and a number of P-40s were caught on the ground here. NARA

Ewa Mooring Mast Field

Ewa Mooring Mast Field seen shortly before the December 7 attack. That morning, the Marine Corps squadrons based there lost a Brewster F2A-3 Buffalo fighter, a number of Grumman F4F Wildcat fighters, nine Douglas SBD Dauntlesses, a Douglas R3D-2 (military designation for the twin-engine DC-5 transport), eight Vought SB2U-3 Vindicators, and one SNJ-3 trainer. In the bottom left is a Grumman F3F biplane fighter and the rows of aircraft are SB2Us in the foreground with SBDs to the right. NARA

A Vought SB2U smolders after the attack. The fabric covering along the fuselage has burned away revealing the aircraft's tubular frame. NARA

This Douglas SBD dive-bomber was caught on the ground at Ewa Field, strafed, and consumed by fire. NARA

Wheeler Army Air Field, Schofield Barracks

Two captured Japanese photographs of the destruction at Wheeler Field. Attacking this airfield virtually guaranteed the Japanese complete air superiority over Oahu. The Japanese benefited from Lt. Gen. Walter C. Short's belief that the greatest danger to his aircraft would come from saboteurs rather from an aerial attack. When the Japanese began strafing Wheeler Field, they found all of the aircraft parked in rows, wingtip to wingtip, which were easy targets for the raiders. The American P-40s can be seen lined up on the Wheeler Field ramp and three Japanese aircraft can be seen, two low having just bombed and strafed the ramp area that are pulling up near the athletic track, and another Val dive-bomber about to push over for an attack. NARA

The U.S. Army's Hawaiian Department was under the command of Lt. Gen. Walter C. Short. Given a temporary promotion from major general to lieutenant general for the Hawaiian Department assignment, he was given an advisory letter written on January 24, 1941, from Secretary of the Navy Frank Knox to Secretary of War Henry L. Stimson, advising that the Pacific Fleet and installations in the Hawaii area were vulnerable to an attack by high-level bombers, a torpedo-plane attack, sabotage, submarine attacks, and ship-based bombardment of shore and harbor installations. Adm. Husband Kimmel was given a copy of the same letter. In spite of having this high-level warning, Short chose to focus on preventing saboteurs from destroying his air arm, leaving his aircraft out on the tarmac, parked in rows, which were easy to guard, but presented a prime target for the Japanese. Subsequent to the letter, Short and Kimmel received a number of warnings, but they all contained mixed messages, often contradicting the previous message. The lasting impression of these messages was that the United States wanted to avoid war, and the failure to send resources to the Hawaiian area reinforced a lack of urgency that war with Japan was imminent. It was only two days before the attack that additional four-engine B-17 bombers were being sent to the Pacific and they were intended for operations in the Philippines. Investigations during and after the war laid blame for the Pearl Harbor disaster at the feet of both Kimmel and Short. It was not until May 1999 that the U.S. Senate passed a symbolic resolution exonerating both Kimmel and Short, but they had both been dead for decades and were unable to see their names cleared. NARA

Soldiers have just removed the serviceable propeller from a burned-out Curtiss P-40 on the ramp at Wheeler Field. The base's Hangar Number Four, background, was virtually undamaged in the air raid. 80-G-32906

Outside Wheeler's Hangar Three, a pair of charred P-40s await clean-up. Notice that many of the window frames in Hangar Three have been removed and stacked against the wall. Shortly after the fires were out, men went to work cleaning up the damage so that repairs could begin. NARA

The doors of Wheeler Field's Hangar One were blown in and fire and bomb damage destroyed a Curtiss P-75 Hawk, right, and heavily damaged a Boeing P-26, facing camera, and a pair of Curtiss P-40s in the background. NARA

In addition to the flight line, the buildings at Schofield Barracks were worked over, receiving heavy damage. NARA

Clean-up of Wheeler Field fell to the men of the 804th Engineer Aviation Battalion, who, at the time, were working at Schofield Barracks and Wheeler Field building anti-aircraft gun emplacements and earthen dispersals to shield aircraft from strafing and bomb splinter damage. Dozens of burned P-40 hulks were bulldozed into piles and removed for recycling. The 804th Engineers later saw action at Saipan and other Central Pacific battles. NARA

Having cleared the tarmac of P-40 hulks, engineers set about surveying the damage to Wheeler Field's aviation infrastructure and the buildings at Schofield Barracks. NARA

Civilian Casualties

Unexploded Japanese bomb found in a cane field after the attack. NARA

There were a number of civilians killed or wounded during the air raid, some from friendly fire. Anti-aircraft shells sometimes failed to detonate at altitude, but would explode when hitting the ground. The man in this car was at the wrong place at the wrong time as a shell exploded near him and shrapnel cut the auto to pieces. The numbers vary between forty-nine and sixty-five killed, and thirty-five wounded. NARA

WAR UPON THE AXIS IS DECLARED

To the Congress of the United States:

Yesterday, December 7, 1941—a date which will live in infamy—the United States of America was suddenly and deliberately attacked by naval and air forces of the Empire of Japan.

The United States was at peace with that Nation and, at the solicitation of Japan, was still in conversation with its Government and its Emperor looking toward the maintenance of peace in the Pacific. Indeed, one hour after Japanese air squadrons had commenced bombing in Oahu, the Japanese Ambassador to the United States and his colleague delivered to the Secretary of State a formal reply to a recent American message. While this reply stated that it seemed useless to continue the existing diplomatic negotiations, it contained no threat or hint of war or armed attack.

It will be recorded that the distance of Hawaii from Japan makes it obvious that the attack was deliberately planned many days or even weeks ago. During the intervening time the Japanese Government had deliberately sought to deceive the United States by false statements and expressions of hope for continued peace.

The attack yesterday on the Hawaiian Islands has caused severe damage to American naval and military forces. Very many American lives have been lost. In addition American ships have been reported torpedoed on the high seas between San Francisco and Honolulu.

Yesterday the Japanese Government also launched an attack against Malaya.

Last night Japanese forces attacked Hong Kong.

Last night Japanese forces attacked Guam.

Last night Japanese forces attacked the Philippine Islands.

Last night the Japanese attacked Wake Island.

Last night the Japanese attacked Midway Island.

Japan has, therefore, undertaken a surprise offensive extending throughout the Pacific area. The facts of yesterday speak for themselves. The people of the United States have already formed their opinions and well understand the implications to the very life and safety of our Nation.

As Commander-in-Chief of the Army and Navy I have directed that all measures be taken for our defense.

Always will we remember the character of the onslaught against us.

No matter how long it may take us to overcome this premeditated invasion, the American people in their righteous might will win through to absolute victory.

I believe I interpret the will of the Congress and of the people when I assert that we will not only defend ourselves to the uttermost but will make very certain that this form of treachery shall never endanger us again.

Hostilities exist. There is no blinking at the fact that our people, our territory, and our interests are in grave danger.

With confidence in our armed forces—with the unbounded determination of our people—we will gain the inevitable triumph—so help us God.

I ask that the Congress declare that since the unprovoked and dastardly attack by Japan on Sunday, December seventh, a state of war has existed between the United States and the Japanese Empire.

Franklin D. Roosevelt
December 8, 1941

CHAPTER 2
FIGHTING AN ENEMY HAVING THE ELEMENT OF SURPRISE

Once the shock of seeing Japanese planes over the harbor wore off, sailors, Marines, and airmen began fighting back. Through the bomb and torpedo explosions ready ammunition lockers were open, sometimes forcefully, and gunners began to fire back at the attackers. At first it was small arms: 45-caliber pistols and various rifles. Then crews began firing back with 50-caliber heavy machine guns, then larger-caliber anti-aircraft cannon. Minesweeper *Avocet* (AVP-4) was one of the first to open fire. She was moored at the Naval Air Station dock, Berth F-1A, and her 3-inch gun crew shot down a Kate that had just put a torpedo into the side of the battleship *California*. This airplane crashed near the base hospital, one of its wings coming to rest near a building. Avocet's gunners accounted for a couple of additional aircraft shot down during the attack.

Crews on board destroyer *Bagley* (DD-386) immediately went into action, breaking open the ready ammunition locker for 50-caliber machine gun belts. The gunners were able to fire on the first three Japanese torpedo bombers during the first wave, and took aim at the attacking Vals in the second. *Bagley* was one of the first American ships to sortie from the harbor in pursuit of the enemy.

Cruisers *Honolulu* (CL-48) and *St. Louis* (CL-49) began opening up with 30-caliber and 50-caliber machine guns and 5-inch/25-caliber guns. Soon nearly every ship in the harbor was taking aim at the Japanese. Typical of the ammunition expended were the numbers from Honolulu: 2,800 rounds of 30-caliber, 4,500 rounds of 50-caliber, and 250 rounds of 5-inch/25-caliber were fired during the attack.

Shortly after the second attack wave arrived over the harbor, seaplane tender *Curtiss* (AV-4) took a bomb hit from a Val that exploded on the main deck, killing twenty-one sailors and wounding fifty-eight men. *Curtiss*'s gunners opened fire on the dive-bombing Vals and scored a direct hit as it pulled up from an attack. The Val's pilot was killed and his plane careened into *Curtiss*, hitting the forward, starboard-side crane. The plane's fuel tank exploded and its wreckage dropped to the boat deck where it burned causing severe damage to the ship's pipes, steam lines, and wiring.

Prior to the December 7 attack, a number of planes and pilots from Wheeler Field were flying gunnery practice missions from Haleiwa Field, twenty miles away on Oahu's north shore. The planes and ground crews remained at the field while the pilots had gone back to Wheeler Field for the weekend. On Saturday night, many of the flyers had made the rounds of the Officers' Clubs at Hickam and Wheeler and had enjoyed themselves late into the morning.

To protect against sabotage, the majority of the aircraft at Wheeler Field were parked on the ramp, wingtip to wingtip, each row only twenty feet from the next. This enabled a small number of armed guards to patrol the perimeter of the parked aircraft to prevent sabotage. On the morning of December 7, almost eighty Curtiss P-36s and P-40s were on the ramp, vulnerable to attack from the air.

At 8:02 a.m., Wheeler Field and the adjacent Schofield Barracks were attacked by twenty-five Val dive-bombers. The Vals dropped bombs on the hangars and returned to strafe aircraft on the ramp as well as the Schofield Barracks area. As the Japanese dive-bombers were working over the airfield, 2nd Lt. George S. Welch and 2nd Lt. Kenneth M. Taylor phoned Haleiwa Field and had their planes armed and engines warmed-up, ready for take off. The two hopped into a car and raced north to Haleiwa Field. Taking off around 8:30 a.m., the pair were instructed to head south toward Ewa Field and the Pearl Harbor area, where they spotted the enemy. Both fliers engaged about a dozen Japanese planes in the skies over Barbers Point with Welch downing two confirmed and one probable and Taylor two.

Out of fuel and ammunition, the pair returned to Wheeler during a lull in the fighting to rearm. Welch was the first back into the air, and as Taylor lifted off, he immediately pursued a Japanese plane passing directly in front of him. While Taylor was firing on the plane ahead of him, a Japanese Zero latched onto his tail and Welch joined the fray, firing at Taylor's pursuer. By the end of the morning, Taylor was credited with two confirmed aerial victories and Welch with four. Taylor and Welch were recognized with the Distinguished Service Cross for their actions that morning.

Between attack waves, two Curtiss P-36s from the 47th Pursuit Squadron and one each from the 45th and 46th Pursuit Squadrons launched from Wheeler Field. Led by 1st Lt. Lewis M. Sanders, the other pilots were 2nd Lt. Othneil Norris, 2nd Lt. John M. Thacker, and 2nd Lt. Philip M. Rasmussen. When Norris got out of his plane and went into the hangar to swap parachutes, 2nd Lt. Gordon H. Sterling Jr. jumped into Norris's P-36. Sterling taxied out and joined the other three P-36s in the flight and joined up on Thacker. Because of Sterling's lack of combat procedures and gunnery training, Sterling was instructed to fly as Sanders's wingman and Thacker and Rasmussen formed the second element. The four P-36s were airborne by 8:50 a.m.

Climbing for altitude, the four P-36s broke out of the clouds near NAS Kaneohe Bay. They immediately spotted six Zeros and dove to attack. Sanders scored the first kill, then saw Sterling pursuing a Zero with another Japanese fighter on his tail. Joining the trio, Sanders started firing at the trailing Zero and this melee was being observed by Rasmussen who reported seeing Sterling's Zero crash into the bay, followed by Sterling. The Zero under fire from Sanders escaped, and it later turned out that the fighter that Sterling was shooting at escaped as well. During this tail chase, Rasmussen had charged his guns, which began to fire uncontrollably. As he was attempting to stop the guns from running away, a Zero flew into the path of his bullets and exploded, earning him an aerial victory credit. Rasmussen then had a pair of Zeros on his tail and he dove for cover in some clouds below him, losing the Japanese fighters in the process.

At Bellows Field, three pilots from the 44th Pursuit Squadron tried to take off during the attack, two of whom lost their lives attempting to repel the attackers. Second Lt. Hans C. Christensen was hit by strafing Japanese planes as he was boarding his P-40 and 2nd Lt. George A. Whiteman took off in a P-40B and was shot down as his plane lifted off the runway. First, Lt. Samuel W. Bishop followed Whiteman into the air, but while climbing for altitude he was hit by machine-gun and 20mm cannon fire from a Zero. Wounded and barely able to control his aircraft, Bishop crashed into the sea off Bellows Field. He was able to swim to shore and eventually returned to duty. All three men received the Silver Star and the Purple Heart.

Crossing over the harbor entrance channel en route to strafe Hickam Field, the Mitsubishi A6M2 Zero fighter flown by Naval Air Pilot first class Takeshi Hirano was heavily damaged by a combination of ground fire and anti-aircraft fire from the destroyer *Helm* and the minesweeper *Bobolink*. To those on the ground, it appeared that Hirano intended on belly landing his Zero on a street inside Fort Kamehameha, which borders the channel entrance to Pearl Harbor. As his crippled fighter sputtered its way over the fort, Hirano's left wing clipped a palm tree, spinning it down to the ground.

The Zero struck at the base of the Ordnance Machine Shop, Building 52, where soldiers had taken cover. The impact of the Japanese fighter killed Hirano instantly. Four soldiers were killed, and five wounded as a result of flying debris from the plane.

As the attack raged overhead, the army and its men bent on souvenir hunting scoured the aircraft for anything valuable. Inside Hirano's pocket was a small map showing the rendezvous point where the retiring attackers would meet as they headed back to the carriers. This gave American search planes a general direction of where the carriers were, but not a precise location of where to expect the Japanese fleet. B-17s went in search of the Japanese, but were unable to locate them.

After the battle, the wreckage was taken to a Hickam Field hangar and studied for its intelligence value. And although nothing new was discovered as far as aerodynamics or weaponry was concerned, investigators deemed that most of it looked like copies of U.S.–made components, giving rise to the belief that the Zero was a copy of an American aircraft.

On the eastern side of Oahu, the morning air over Naval Air Station Kaneohe Bay was pierced by the rumble of low-flying aircraft around 7:50 a.m. Soon thereafter the attackers were strafing aircraft moored in the bay and those on the seaplane ramp. Sailors and Marines began to fire back with rifles and machine guns. The attack lasted between ten and fifteen minutes before the aircraft retired to the north.

The second attack wave did more damage to the base, this time dropping small bombs in addition to strafing the navy Catalinas. A direct hit on Hangar No. 1 did tremendous damage to the building and completely destroyed four PBYs inside. The majority of Kaneohe Bay's casualties occurred in the moored aircraft or as crews were trying to launch or move the big flying boats.

Anti-aircraft gunners at Kaneohe Bay were able to score a number of hits as three or four aircraft were seen leaving the area streaming fuel. They were able to confirm one Japanese aircraft as shot down, that belonging to Lt. Fusata Iida, leader of *Soryu* fighter unit's attack on the naval air station. Iida, realizing he would not be able to make it back to the carrier had committed himself to crashing his aircraft into a high-value target should something go wrong. Having rejoined his flight, he signaled his intentions, then rolled his aircraft and dove toward the air station firing his guns on the way down. Iida crashed into a hill one mile north of the hangar line. He was buried the next day with full military honors in the same plot as the fifteen men from the air station who perished in the attack.

Another Zero pilot unable to make the return trip to his carrier was Airman First Class Shigenori Nishikaichi from *Hiryu*. Having been struck by anti-aircraft fire during the raid, Nishikaichi headed for the rendezvous with the Japanese aircraft carriers. He was accompanied by another *Hiryu* fighter, but ran out of fuel over Niihau and crash-landed. The second aircraft continued to the west and was never seen by the islanders again.

Six days after the Pearl Harbor attack, on Saturday, December 13, six men rowed from Niihau to Waimea, Kauai, to report the crash landing and subsequent capture of Airman Shigenori Nishikaichi. At the time, there was no communication with Niihau and no radio to inform the islanders that America was now at war with Japan. On Kauai, the authorities were notified and twelve soldiers from Company M, 299th Infantry, were sent back to Niihau on board the lighthouse tender *Kukui*. In addition to the men from Company M, the *Kukui* carried an additional dozen armed men and two heavy machine guns. The *Kukui* departed Waimea at 6 p.m. local time and arrived at the southern tip of Niihau at 7:30 a.m. The men disembarked, had breakfast, then began the ten-mile march to the Nonopapa village where the Japanese pilot was being held.

The troops arrived at 1:50 p.m. to learn that the Zero fighter had been burned by its pilot, who was dead, and to hear a bizarre story about the past six days since the Japanese fighter crashed on the island, which resulted in the pilot attempting to send a radio message from the Zero's cockpit, him burning the plane, a native Hawaiian being shot, the pilot being picked up and being bodily thrown into a stone wall resulting in a crushed skull, and a native Japanese worker who had aided the pilot committing suicide. The week's events became known as "The Niihau Incident."

In all, twenty-nine Japanese planes and their crews did not return to the carriers. Nine of the aircraft were Zeros, fifteen Val dive-bombers, and five were Kate torpedo-bombers.

Two D3A1 Val dive-bombers circle the crash site of Val B11-233 from *Shokaku*. This photo was shot by T/Sgt. Lee Embree, who was a passenger on an out-of-fuel B-17E making an approach to Hickam Field. As the bomber passed One'ula Beach, two D3A1 Val dive-bombers are seen circling the Val's crash site. The corner of Ewa Field can be seen in the left center of the photograph. An SBD dive-bomber from *Enterprise* crashed in the same area at nearly the same time. NARA

Wing of a Nakajima Type 97 Kate torpedo-bomber from *Kaga* that crashed at the Pearl Harbor base hospital. This aircraft scored a torpedo hit on the battleship *California* before being shot out of the sky by gunners on board the minesweeper *Avocet*. All five Kates destroyed in the attack were shot down during the first wave by anti-aircraft fire and all were based aboard *Kaga*. As can be seen from the missing metal, souvenir hunters have stripped the Japanese Hinomaru meatball insignia from the wing. NH 50940

Flames race back from the wing of a Val dive-bomber hit by anti-aircraft fire over Pearl Harbor. Seven Vals were shot down by anti-aircraft fire during the second attack wave. NARA

Aerial view showing Haleiwa Auxiliary Field on Oahu's north shore, where a number of aircraft from Wheeler Field had been temporarily based for a training exercise. When the Japanese attacked Wheeler Field, 2nd Lt. Kenneth M. Taylor and 2nd Lt. George S. Welch drove the twenty miles to Haleiwa, jumped into two waiting P-40s, and joined the melee of attacking aircraft above Pearl Harbor area. NARA

Nine Japanese planes were shot down during the attack by Wheeler-based pilots, from left: 2nd Lt. Harry W. Brown, 2nd Lt. Philip M. Rasmussen, 2nd Lt. Kenneth M. Taylor, 2nd Lt. George S. Welch, and 1st Lt. Lewis M. Sanders. Taylor was credited with two confirmed aerial victories and Welch with four. Second Lt. Gordon H. Sterling Jr. was flying a P-36 and was credited with a kill before he, too, was shot down. Sterling was in a tail chase firing at a *Hiryu* Zero when another fighter got onto his tail. Seeing that Sterling was in trouble, Sanders dove after the trailing Zero and the four aircraft dove into a cloudbank. When Sanders emerged, he was alone in the sky. Thinking that the three aircraft in front of him had flown into the sea, Sterling was credited with an aerial victory. Postwar records show that the two attacking Zeros from *Hiryu* returned to the carrier. SIGNAL CORPS

Naval Air Pilot, first class, Takeshi Hirano's Zero (tail code AI-154) was shot down by fire from shore-based small-arms and anti-aircraft from *Helm* (DD-388) and *Bobolink* (AM-20). Hirano's Zero clipped a palm tree, which forced his aircraft to crash at the base of Building 52, the Ordnance Machine Shop killing Hirano and four Americans. Extensive damage to the left wing can be seen in this photo. SIGNAL CORPS

Hirano's Zero separated into three pieces, with the engine and empennage splitting off on both sides of the aircraft's center section. 80-G-13040

Upon closer inspection of the Zero's cockpit, it was determined that the fighter was fitted with a Fairchild Radio Compass, model RC-4. 80-G-22158

One of the outer wing panels of Hirano's AI-154 rests against the Ordnance Machine Shop building. The Zero's landing gear can be seen retracted into the wing in the foreground. SIGNAL CORPS

Hirano's Zero was taken to a hangar on Hickam Field, and each shop was given the opportunity to inspect the fighter and assess its technical aspects. Once each shop had written its reports, the fighter was shipped to Wright Field, Dayton, Ohio, for further inspection. SIGNAL CORPS

George Welch shot down a *Kaga* Aichi D3A2 Type 99 Val dive-bomber that came to rest at 711 Neal Street, three quarters of a mile from the end of the Wheeler Field runway. The landing gear leg that forks over the wheel can be seen in the lower right of the photo identifying the plane as a Val. The chain-link fence seen in the upper left near the propeller surrounds the local electrical substation. NARA

One of the *Kaga* Vals that was shot down by anti-aircraft fire crashed south of battleship *California*, seen in top photo at left, near Berth F-2. After lifting the dive-bomber from the harbor bottom, it, too, was studied for its intelligence value. 80-G-32441

This Kate torpedo-bomber recovered from inside Pearl Harbor has been identified as AII-356 from *Kaga* and was flown by Lt. Mitsumori Suzuki. Each Kate carried a crew of three. NARA

Sailors and airmen killed in the attack on Naval Air Station Kaneohe Bay were laid to rest in the sand dunes at the northeast side of the base. Sailors are shown placing the coffin of Aviation Machinist's Mate First Class Robert K. Porterfield. KANEOHE TOWN LIBRARY

Fifteen caskets line the mass grave of the Americans killed during the December 7 attack on Kaneohe Bay. The base's Marine detachment formed the honor guard, which is about to render a salute while bugler Theodore J. Moss stands at attention at the head of the grave. KANEOHE TOWN LIBRARY

After concluding the ceremony for the American dead, Chaplain Lt. Wallace L. Kennedy (right, back to camera) offered a prayer for Lt. Fusata Iida from the carrier *Soryu*, who died when he crashed his Zero onto the air station. Fusata was aiming to crash his crippled Zero into one of the air station's hangars but missed his target.

KANEOHE TOWN LIBRARY

During the war years, Iida's grave was marked with a simple sign and a Japanese flag. His remains were returned to Japan after the war.

KANEOHE TOWN LIBRARY

Unable to make it back to the carrier
Hiryu, Petty Officer First Class
Shigenori Nishikaichi landed on the
island of Niihau. 80-G-22162

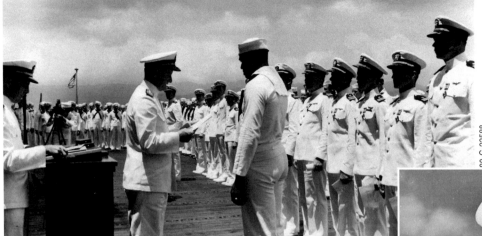

80-G-23588

Mess Attendant, second class, Doris Miller was awarded the Navy Cross by Adm. Chester W. Nimitz, in a May 27, 1942, ceremony aboard the *Enterprise* while docked at Pearl Harbor. After torpedoes had struck the *West Virginia*, Miller ran to his battle station at an anti-aircraft battery magazine amidships only to find it destroyed. After assisting officers who were attending to *West Virginia*'s wounded captain, Mervyn Bennion, Miller was ordered to help Lt. Frederic H. White and Ens. Victor Delano load a 50-cal machine gun. The officers were distracted and Miller began firing at incoming aircraft. When the gun ran out of ammunition, Miller helped move Captain Bennion to the navigation bridge. He then moved a number of other wounded sailors to the quarterdeck where they were able to get medical treatment, thus saving their lives. "Dorie" Miller was the first African-American to be awarded the Navy Cross. He perished on November 24, 1943, while serving aboard the escort carrier *Liscome Bay* (CVE-56), which was torpedoed by the Japanese submarine *I-175* near Makin Island in the Gilbert Islands.

80-G-408456

Brig. Gen Barney McKinney Giles, 4th Air Force commanding general, presented Purple Hearts to seven Army Air Forces members wounded during the Pearl Harbor attack. From left, facing the general, front row, are Pfc. Garrett C. Tyra, Ysleta, Texas; Lt. Joseph T. Moore, Clinton, Indiana; Sgt. Raymond Mayo, Guin, Alabama; and Lt. Walter S. Smith III, Mill Valley, California. Second row: Lt. Marston C. Reed, Torrington, Wyoming; Lt. Russell O. McKray, Kalona, Iowa; and Pvt. Ben Odetta, Avenal, California. The certificates these men received read, in part, "having performed meritorious acts of essential service during the Japanese attack on the Island of Oahu, Territory of Hawaii, December 7, 1941." Of interest, the Army Air Corps became the Army Air Forces on March 9, 1942, and Giles was promoted to the rank of brigadier general that same month. These medals were awarded while the injured men were recuperating at hospitals in the San Francisco, California, area. USAAF

CHAPTER 3
FLEET SALVAGE

While the Japanese were still overhead, sailors began the task of rescuing survivors from the water and organizing the effort to free men trapped in the overturned hulls of *Oklahoma* and *Utah*. When the smoke cleared, there were eighteen ships and a floating dry dock sunk or seriously damaged: battleships *Arizona, California, Maryland, Nevada, Oklahoma, Pennsylvania, Tennessee, West Virginia;* cruisers *Honolulu and Raleigh;* destroyers *Cassin, Downes,* and *Shaw;* and the seaplane tender *Curtiss,* minelayer *Oglala,* tug *Sotoyomo,* target ship *Utah,* repair ship *Vestal,* and floating dry dock *YFD-2.*

The harbor was a mess. Oil fouled the water. There was flaming oil spreading across the surface and there were men in the water, many injured. Nearly a dozen ships were beached or sitting on the bottom; two were inverted. There was death and destruction all around.

As men were being pulled from the water and sent from ship to ship or to shore, the injured were being transported to the base hospital and makeshift medical centers around the base. At the berths around Ford Island, the immediate need was for tools and torches to begin the rescue of those trapped within *Oklahoma* and *Utah.*

On the overturned hull of *Oklahoma,* Lt. Cmdr. William M. Hobby Jr. and Boatswain Adolph M. Bothne were joined by Cmdr. E. Kranzfelder, Lt. Cmdr. William L. Benson, and Lt. Cmdr. Harry H. Henderson, along with thirty to forty sailors. The group began discussing how to rescue the men trapped within the hull below. Kranzfelder, who was on the staff of Commander Battleships, detailed the immediate action taken to contact the men within the hull:

> Lines were rigged from [*Oklahoma*'s] bilge keel at intervals along the bottom, and telephone communication was established with the *Maryland.* An air supply line was quickly rigged from the *Maryland* to the *Oklahoma,* strainers were removed from main injections and overboard discharge [ports] in an attempt to gain access to the engine room. Contact was established with two men entrapped in the evaporator pump room through a small overboard discharge connection in the hull. Food and water

was passed down to these men. From information obtained from these men as to their location in the ship and with the aid of [*Oklahoma*'s] booklet of plans it was possible to determine the best locations to cut access holes in the ship's bottom. Since practically the entire bottom of the *Oklahoma* consists of oil tanks, with the exception of the reserve feed bottoms, considerable care had to be exercised in cutting holes with an oxyacetylene torch in order not to open holes in the bottom, which would permit the egress of oil with the attendant fire hazard.

To gain access to the interior of the ship, ten holes were cut in the bottom of *Oklahoma*'s hull at Frames 27-28, 30-31, 61-62, 76-77, 100-101, 116, 129-130, and 133-134 (measured from the bow, the distance between each frame is four feet; *Oklahoma*'s overall length is 583 feet, and thus Frame 27-28 would be 108 feet aft of the bow). At first cutting torches were used to gain entry to the hull, but it was soon determined that the torches were consuming all of the oxygen in the small, interior spaces, so rescuers switched to pneumatic chipping hammers. One man emerged from the bottom of the hull on December 7, thirty more the following day, and the last man on December 9; thirty-two in all, while 429 officers and men perished in the attack.

SENT TO THE WEST COAST

Some ships could be repaired at the Pearl Harbor Navy Yard and returned to service while others would be made seaworthy and sent to the U.S. West Coast for extensive repairs and modernization. Washington State's Puget Sound Naval Shipyard and California's Mare Island Naval Shipyard had the facilities and the capacity to quickly address the damage on each ship, update its systems, and send it back to fight the Japanese.

Battleships *Pennsylvania, Maryland,* and *Tennessee* were attended to in quick succession. *Pennsylvania* was struck by bombs, one of which killed a crew manning a 5-inch/51-caliber gun. Fifteen men on board *Pennsylvania* were killed, along with fourteen missing in action and thirty-eight wounded. She was readied for sea by December 12 and sailed from Pearl Harbor eight days later for further repairs and modernization at San Francisco. On April 23, the battleship rejoined the fight against the Japanese in the Aleutian Islands.

Maryland was moored inboard of *Oklahoma* and escaped the attentions of the Japanese during the air raid. She was struck by a pair of bombs, but damage to her was light in comparison to ships moored near her. The battleship sailed for the Puget Sound Naval Shipyard, arriving on December 30. She was back sailing with the fleet on February 26, 1942, supporting operations in the New Hebrides.

When the air raid began, *Tennessee* was moored inside *West Virginia* behind *Oklahoma* and *Maryland* and ahead of *Arizona*. When *West Virginia* sank at her moorings, she trapped *Tennessee* against the quays of Berth F-6. Protected from torpedo attack by the sunken hull of *West Virginia*, *Tennessee* received two bomb hits from Japanese horizontal bombers. The first bomb penetrated Turret Number Three, but broke up as it cut through the decks igniting a fire. The second bomb struck the center gun of Turret Number Two, exploding on contact. Shrapnel from the bomb killed the commander of nearby *West Virginia*, Capt. Mervyn S. Bennion. Flaming oil on the surface of Battleship Row caused a number of fires on board *Tennessee*. Although trapped, *Tennessee*'s engines were run ahead and the wash from the propellers helped alter the course of the flaming oil on the surface of the harbor coming from *Arizona*. In addition, sailors on board *Tennessee* used fire hoses to keep the oil fires away from the battleship's stern. Just over a week after the attack, the mooring quay holding *Tennessee* was removed, and she steamed past capsized *Oklahoma* and into dry dock on December 16. She then sailed to the Puget Sound Naval Shipyard for repairs and modernization. *Tennessee* returned to the fleet on February 26, 1942.

Light cruiser *Honolulu* received minimal damage from a bomb's near-miss and was quickly repaired while the *Raleigh* was struck by a torpedo amidships, below the armor belt on the port side, during the first wave. Damage from the exploding torpedo caused the forward boiler rooms and the forward engine room to flood. In jeopardy of capsizing, the order was given to lighten the ship on the port side. Everything loose was thrown overboard. To add to the misery, a Japanese dive-bomber took aim on the light cruiser and sent a bomb into her deck. Fortunately, the bomb passed through three decks and out the side of the cruise to explode in the mud of the harbor bottom. Concussion from the bomb opened hull plates around Frame 112.

Due to the construction of the ship, counter-flooding was not much of an option and a barge was tied along side to maintain buoyancy. After repairs in the Navy Yard that made her seaworthy, *Raleigh* was sent to Mare Island Naval Shipyard in California to complete the job. She rejoined the fleet on July 23, 1942, escorting ships between San Francisco and the Fiji Islands.

The *Mahan*-class destroyer *Shaw* was on board floating dry dock *YFD-2* at the time of the attack. She was the focus of three dive-bombers from the second wave of Japanese attackers. Bombs dropped by the first two Vals started fires in the bow and on the main deck. The third Val's bomb exploded below decks rupturing a fuel oil tank and igniting its contents as they sprayed out through the shrapnel holes. The fire became uncontrollable and its heat cooked off the munitions in the ship's forward magazine. The resulting explosion severed *Shaw*'s bow, laying it twisted to starboard on the floor of the floating dry dock. In an effort to extinguish the fire, *YFD-2* was flooded which made the aft section of *Shaw* buoyant, enabling it to float aft, partially freeing it from the dry dock.

Shaw's hull aft of the bridge was in good condition and the decision was made to remove the mangled sections and replace them with a temporary bow. This would enable *Shaw* to sail to the U.S. West Coast, where a new bow would be fitted at the Mare Island Naval Shipyard. After major surgery and modernization, *Shaw* returned to the fleet at Pearl Harbor on August 31, 1942, to serve as a convoy escort. She then helped take the fight to the Japanese at her first major engagement at the Battle of the Santa Cruz Islands.

The district harbor tug *Sotoyomo* (YT-9) was sitting in *YFD-2* ahead of destroyer *Shaw* when the attack began. Shrapnel and fire from the explosion of *Shaw*'s forward magazine saw *Sotoyomo* sink when the floating dry dock was submerged. In the aftermath of the attack, *Sotoyomo* was adopted by the men of Pearl Harbor Repair and Salvage Unit, who restored the 230-ton, 97-foot-long tug, and had her back in service by August 1942. Returning to the fleet in October of that year, *Sotoyomo* served in New Caledonia, Guadalcanal, and the Philippines. Wartime service had been hard on the tug and she was considered in poor condition. She was scuttled near Leyte, Philippines, in February 1946.

YFD-2 was attacked by five Val dive-bombers during the second wave, and with *Shaw* on fire and *Sotoyomo* burning as a result of the destroyer's fuel fire, the floating dry dock was submerged to keep her from being consumed by fire. Shrapnel from the bombs and the explosion of *Shaw*'s forward magazine holed the floating dry dock. It took divers nearly a month to patch 155 holes in the hull before they could refloat her. On January 25, 1942, *YFD-2* returned to operations with destroyer *Shaw* first to receive her attentions. Final repairs were made to *YFD-2* on May 15, 1942, and she was marked as fully operational.

Seaplane tender *Curtiss* was in the thick of things on the western side of Ford Island, having spotted and fired upon a midget submarine, then being struck by an out-of-control Japanese Val dive-bomber followed by three near-miss bomb hits and one that exploded on the main deck. Shrapnel from the bombs did a tremendous amount of damage, not to the seaplane tender's hull, but to the aircraft repair infrastructure and shops on board the ship. *Curtiss* was initially repaired in late December 1941, and once specific replacement parts arrived from the mainland, she returned to the Navy Yard for final repairs beginning on April 26, 1942.

Repair ship *Vestal* was alongside *Arizona* when the air raid began, tied portside to portside with the battleship. *Vestal*'s 5-inch gun began engaging low-flying planes immediately, supplemented by its 3-inch gun, which fired three rounds before it jammed. As the gun crew was working to clear the cannon, *Arizona*'s forward magazine exploded. Two bombs dropped by dive-bombers struck the ship, one forward that exploded below decks in a storage room, and one that passed through the ship exploding underneath. The second bomb's hole and the concussion from its explosion saw the ship take on a great deal of water causing a seven-degree list to port. As fires spread on the surface of the harbor, tugs helped *Vestal* anchor a safe distance to the north, but the amount of flooding dictated that the ship be beached until repair facilities could be made available.

When the first wave struck, destroyer *Helm* (DD-388) was able to escape the harbor and took up station southeast of the entrance. During the second wave, a Val spotted her alone five miles south of the Honolulu Harbor entrance and dropped a pair of 250-kilogram bombs, which missed but exploded close-in. The near-misses produced large concussion waves that caused flooding in the forward hull area. Pearl Harbor Navy Yard technicians repaired the ship in five days, between January 15 and 20, 1942.

HEAVY SALVAGE EFFORTS

The ships requiring greater technical attention and resources before they could return to the fleet included destroyers *Cassin* and *Downes*, battleships *Nevada*, *California*, *West Virginia*, and *Utah* and the minelayer *Oglala*.

Cassin and *Downes* were sitting at the head of empty Dry Dock Number One undergoing repair when the air raid started. *Cassin* slipped off of its keel blocks, and *Downes* was heavily damaged by fire from both ships. *Downes* was too heavily damaged to repair at the Pearl Harbor Navy Yard, and it was doubtful she could economically be made seaworthy for the long journey to a shipyard on the West Coast.

The decision was made to salvage as much of the machinery from *Downes* as possible and ship it to the Mare Island Naval Shipyard, where it would be installed into a new hull, also named *Downes* and designated DD-375. The new *Downes* was re-commissioned on November 15, 1943, and rejoined the fleet on March 8, 1944.

Cassin was righted and made seaworthy for the tow to the Mare Island Naval Shipyard. Here she was rebuilt, re-commissioned on February 6, 1944, and returned to the fleet on April 22 in time to participate in the attacks on Saipan.

Battleship *Nevada* was struck by a torpedo at Frame 41 (between Turrets Number One and Two) during the first attack wave at approximately 8:10 a.m. The ship started to list to port, but counter-flooding corrected it. During the lull between attacks, *Nevada* attempted to make for open water during the air raid. When the second wave began, Japanese aircraft saw the potential of sinking *Nevada* in the harbor channel and began to concentrate their attack on the battleship as she passed in front of 1010 Dock. *Nevada* was struck by five 250-kilogram bombs, all landing within the span of one or two minutes; the exact order the bombs hit was not recorded. One bomb passed through the main deck and exited the ship at Frame 15, exploding in the harbor; its concussion split open some of the hull plate seams causing flooding. A second bomb dropped straight to the bottom of the ship near the bow, exploding near a gasoline tank at Frame 7. A third bomb entered the superstructure, bounced off the armored second deck and detonated amidships causing heavy damage; a fourth bomb exploded in the center of the ship at the base of the smoke stack; and a fifth bomb detonated on the upper deck near Frame 80. Fire on the main and second decks near the bow burned for two days.

Ordered not to attempt to exit the harbor, *Nevada* was first run aground at Hospital Point, at the western most end of the Navy Yard. The battleship was creating a choke point between it and Ford Island and a pair of tugs (*Hoga* and *YT-130*) pushed on *Nevada*'s stern until the bow became free. The tugs then assisted *Nevada* across the channel and grounded her, stern on, to coral ledge on Waipio Peninsula. It was here that the iconic photos of the tug *Hoga* spraying water onto the ship's bow fires was taken. In the grounding, *Nevada*'s starboard propeller was damaged as her stern sat on the ledge while the bow of the ship floated. Fires raged and flooding continued while the ship's pumps and damage control crews attempted to stem the incoming water.

While salvage work was underway, crews began to lighten the ship removing ammunition, cleaning spaces as the water level dropped, securing holes, making the interior watertight, and removing as much of the electrical equipment as possible and sending it for overhaul so that it would be ready for re-installation when the ship was in dry dock. Small patches, known as "window frame" patches were manufactured in the Navy Yard and installed on the hull by divers. A month of effort was spent trying to fit a patch made for *Nevada*'s sister ship *Oklahoma* to cover the 48-foot-long by 25-foot-tall hole made by the torpedo strike. It was then determined that *Nevada*'s transverse bulkheads surrounding the torpedo hole would hold and the ship could be towed across the harbor to Dry Dock Number Two.

The battleship was dry-docked on February 18, 1942. Divers from *Nevada*, minesweepers *Widgeon* (AM-22) and *Ortolan* (AM-45), Destroyer Repair Unit at Pearl Harbor, and the Pacific Bridge Company made more than 400 dives, spending over 1,500 hours underwater to patch the battleship and make her ready to transit the harbor. *Nevada* was released from the dry dock on March 15, and sailed for the Puget Sound Naval Shipyard for overhaul and modernization on April 22, arriving nine days later.

Battleship *California* took two torpedoes into her port side below the armor belt (at Frames 52 and 101) and suffered a direct bomb hit on the upper deck at Frame 59 on the starboard side. Two other bombs were near misses. In addition to her own damage, fuel oil on the harbor surface was burning, with *California* right in its path. In the hours after the attack, the burning fuel oil engulfed the ship combined with fires started by the bomb hit soon required the crew to temporarily abandon ship. Flooding was a slow, losing battle and in spite of the crew's valiant efforts, *California* settled to the harbor bottom in the early evening of December 10, 1941.

Using the ship's watertight bulkheads to advantage, *California* was unwatered and refloated without using external hull patches. Cofferdams attached to the main deck ensured the ship had plenty of freeboard during the tow across the harbor and could not be swamped, thereby blocking the channel. This was the most expedient way to get the ship from the harbor into dry dock and eventually back into service. *California* was refloated on March 24, 1942, and entered Dry Dock Number Two on April 9. On October 20, 1942, *California* left Pearl Harbor for the Puget Sound Naval Shipyard for modernization.

West Virginia is thought to have taken seven torpedo hits, but the exact number was never determined due to the damage sustained. Three aerial torpedoes impacted the battleship below the armor belt, while another one tested the belt's ability to withstand a direct explosion. One, maybe two, torpedoes entered *West Virginia* through holes made be previous torpedoes. These exploded deep inside the ship causing considerable damage. Essentially, the torpedoes had opened the port side of the ship from stem to stern. Patches were needed from Frame 43 to 52 and from 61.5 to 97.5—a combined distance of approximately 180 feet.

In addition to the torpedo damage, two 16-inch artillery shells, converted into aerial bombs, were dropped on *West Virginia*. Luckily, neither detonated. Fires were a severe problem, with flaming fuel oil washing into the ship from *Arizona* coupled with fires within the battleship itself. Like on other ships salvaged within the harbor, hull patches sealed with underwater concrete stemmed the inflow of water, enabling pumps to begin the unwatering process. More than 650 tons of concrete were needed to seal the patches. To lighten the ship, 800,000 gallons of fuel oil was pumped from *West Virginia*'s tanks and the powder and shells for her 16-inch main guns were removed. On May 17, 1942, *West Virginia* was floating and was moved into Dry Dock Number One on June 9. A little less than one year later, on May 7, 1943, *West Virginia* sailed under her own power to the Puget Sound Naval Shipyard for modernization and updating of her armament.

On the morning of the attack, minelayer *Oglala* was tied to the light cruiser *Helena* at Berth 2 on 1010 Dock with an eight-foot gap between the ships. During the first torpedo plane attack, at approximately 8 a.m., a torpedo passed under *Oglala* and struck the light cruiser. The underwater concussion from the torpedo blast coupled with the bomb's near miss in the same area between the ships moments later split the minesweeper's hull plates. *Oglala*'s crew were able to secure the fires in the boilers, exit the fire rooms closing the watertight doors behind them, and get above decks.

Within thirty minutes, *Oglala* had taken on a five-degree list to port and was taking on water in her stern. The tugs *Hoga* and *YT-130* moved the minesweeper away from Helena and tied her up to 1010 Dock. By 9:30 a.m., *Oglala* was listing 20 degrees to port and, moments before 10 a.m., was on the harbor bottom. She was deemed a complete loss, but that decision was later reversed. *Oglala* would live to sail another day. A team of eighteen divers patched the minelayer's hull, ran lifting chains through the mud, and removed most of the ship's upper structure to prepare her for righting. On April 11, 1942, the first attempt failed when the lifting chains came loose. She was righted on April 23. Now upright, a cofferdam was installed to enable the ship to be dewatered. After three attempts to refloat the minesweeper, *Oglala* was dry-docked in July 1942. After repairs, she was sent to the West Coast for modernization and conversion to an internal combustion engine repair ship. Re-commissioned in February 1944, *Oglala* sailed for the waters off New Guinea in April 1944.

Three ships with naval careers ended by the Japanese were battleships *Arizona* and *Oklahoma*, along with the target ship *Utah*. All three met a violent end, with the forward magazine of *Arizona* exploding with the force of one megaton, while *Oklahoma* and *Utah* were holed by torpedoes, subsequently capsizing.

Battleship *Arizona* was moored to Berth F-7, bow pointing southeast, with the repair ship *Vestal* tied alongside, port-to-port. Within fifteen minutes of the start of the attack, the battleship's forward magazine exploded with devastating results, pushing out the sides of the hull, collapsing the forward decks, and dropping Turret Number One two decks down. The majority of the *Arizona*'s 1,177 officers and men that perished during the attack were killed the instant the magazine exploded.

The battleship was too far-gone to be saved; however, it still held many parts valuable for the war effort. The battleship's anti-aircraft guns as well as her 14-inch main batteries and all of the ammunition on board were salvaged, refurbished, and reissued to the fleet. The guns from Turrets Three and Four were given to the U.S. Army for use as coastal defense batteries in the hills overlooking the approaches to Pearl Harbor. Today, more than 1,100 men are entombed inside *Arizona*'s hull and a memorial spans the width of the ship.

The largest recovery effort in the wake of the Pearl Harbor attack was the righting and raising of the battleship *Oklahoma*. The Pacific Bridge Company of San Francisco was brought in to assist the Pearl Harbor Navy Yard's salvage staff in the recovery effort. One of the company's greatest contributions was convincing the Navy to use hull patches sealed with underwater concrete, rather than attempting to build cofferdams around each sunken ship. The patch/concrete repair method accelerated the time it took to get the ships off the harbor bottom and into dry dock for repairs.

Divers made the inverted hull watertight and cut off much of the battleship's superstructure. The majority of the 5-inch ammunition was removed along with the ship's propellers. Once this was complete, the interior was pumped full of compressed air, blowing out a large portion of the water inside the ship. This air bubble lightened the ship by approximately 20,000 tons, thereby reducing the force needed to pull the ship upright.

Soil tests showed that the mid- and aft-parts of the ship were in relatively thick clay that would hold the battleship as she rolled. However, the bow section was in loose mud, which would allow the ship to slide toward the winches on Ford Island. To ensure a solid footing for the rolling maneuver, 2,200 tons of coal were poured along the inverted bow section to provide a gripping surface when the ship turned.

Wooden righting bents were attached to the fuselage and steel wires were attached to lugs welded to *Oklahoma*'s hull at the frame lines. The wires were strung to a block and tackle system that gave a seventeen-times pulling advantage to each of the 429-ton capacity winches, twenty-one in all, which were installed on Ford Island. The pulling operation got underway on March 8, 1943, and it took seventy-four days to right the battleship.

Having rolled upright, a patch was delivered to *Oklahoma* that would cover the largest section of damage, from Frames 43 to 75. Other smaller patches were installed, each sealed with underwater concrete. It took twenty pumps, each with a capacity of moving 10,000 gallons per minute, eleven hours to dewater the ship making her buoyant again. She floated on November 3, 1943.

Once raised, *Oklahoma* was moved to Dry Dock Number Two on December 28, 1943. Here she was stripped of all valuable components, made watertight, and officially decommissioned on September 1, 1944. The once-proud battleship was now a hulk and she sat in the harbor until after the war when the hulk was sold for its scrap value. Moore Shipbuilding and Drydock of Oakland, California, won the right to scrap the hulk on December 5, 1946, paying $46,000 for the privilege. Two tugs escorted the hulk of *Oklahoma* out of Pearl Harbor en route to the West Coast on May 10, 1947. She never completed the journey to the breakers, as *Oklahoma* slipped under the waves in a storm one week later.

Utah, moored at Berth F-11 on the west side of Ford Island, took a torpedo hit in the bow and capsized in minutes. With the hull inverted, sailors could hear men trapped inside tapping on the hull. A rescue attempt was quickly organized with a cutting torch brought over from the light cruise *Raleigh*, which had its own troubles. Ten men were rescued from the overturned ship, with sixty-four having perished in the attack and subsequent capsizing.

Having been commissioned in August 1911, *Utah* and its 12-inch main guns were antiquated by the end of the 1920s. In 1931, the battleship was stripped of its armament and converted to a target ship (designated AG-16). As she lay on the bottom of Pearl Harbor in an out-of-the-way berth, *Utah* was stripped of its accessible and usable parts; then came the discussion about whether or not to spend the money to remove the wreck.

Plans were made to salvage *Utah* using the same methods and equipment as was used on righting *Oklahoma*. In late spring 1943, winches were installed on Ford Island and the attempt to roll the former battleship started in June of that year. *Utah* was rolled to 38-degrees, but then she dragged across the harbor bottom. Unable to continue the recovery, *Utah* was left *in situ* as a memorial to those who perished on her and those who died in the attack. The hulk can be seen on the western side of Ford Island with prior arrangement.

Although many paid the ultimate price at Pearl Harbor, a great effort was begun at the Navy Yard to recover from the surprise attack and return damaged ships to the fleet. This restoration effort then stretched to the West Coast shipyards where damaged battleships, cruisers, destroyers, and auxiliaries were further repaired and modernized. These ships would eventually take the fight to the Japanese home islands. As the shock of the attack was realized and the battle began on the home front, the slogan, "Remember Pearl Harbor" became the rallying cry for a nation.

After the attack, *Arizona* (right) continues to burn while *West Virginia* sits on the bottom, with *Tennessee* to its rear. A barge is alongside capsized *Oklahoma*, aiding in the rescue effort as men work to cut holes in the battleship's bottom plates to reach trapped sailors. *Maryland* remains tied to its berth inside *Oklahoma*. 80-G-32596

Battleship Row seen from the air on December 10, 1941, three days after the air raid. The five aviation fuel tanks on Ford Island were untouched. These were the tanks that had been replenished by oiler *Neosho* before the air raid. *California* sits on the bottom at Berth F-3, left, with *Oklahoma*'s inverted hull to the right outside *Maryland* at Berth F-5. Sunken *West Virginia* and heavily damaged *Tennessee* are at Berth F-6 with *Arizona* at F-7 streaming oil into the harbor. Notice how the oil flows from *Arizona*'s ruptured tanks streaming between Battleship Row and Ford Island. This photo illustrates how burning fuel oil would have quickly engulfed *Tennessee*'s stern and cut off the escape route for many sailors in the water trying to swim to safety at Ford Island. 80-G-387565 / NH 57670

Captain Homer N. Wallin (left) was on board *California* when the Japanese attack began. In early 1942, he was appointed commanding officer of the Pearl Harbor Navy Yard's Salvage Division and was responsible for raising and repairing the majority of ships damaged in the attack. Wallin is seen on board *West Virginia* with Lt. Cmdr. William White, its commanding officer, during the salvage and repair effort (December 7, 1941, to November 15, 1942). Both men are clad in "tank" suits and rubber boots for working in the oily sludge below decks. NH 64490

Pennsylvania

Smoke continues to pour from *Arizona* and frames Dry Dock No. 1 with *Pennsylvania* and destroyers *Downes* and *Cassin* resting against her. During the attack, Dry Dock No. 1 was flooded to prevent further damage to the ships should a Japanese bomb penetrate the dry dock's door. Damaged cruiser *Helena* can be seen to the right near the crane, tied to 1010 Dock. 80-G-19943

Aerial view of the harbor's dry dock area showing *Pennsylvania, Cassin,* and *Downes* in Dry Dock No. 1, and cruiser *Helena* in Dry Dock No. 2 preparing to have its torpedo damage addressed; Dry Dock No. 3 is vacant, while floating dry dock *YFD-2* is partially submerged, with destroyer *Shaw* and tug *Sotoyomo* sunk inside. The dark areas on the harbor's surface are fuel oil from ships sunk during the attack. 80-G-387598

Pennsylvania's bow shows the fire damage from the burning *Cassin* and *Downes* as well as oil from the destroyers that burned on the water's surface. Technicians at the Pearl Harbor Navy Yard quickly replaced *Pennsylvania*'s shafts and propellers and a damaged 5-inch/51-caliber gun with the same unit from *West Virginia*. The battleship was out of dry dock by December 12 and departed the Navy Yard on December 20 for San Francisco, where she underwent further repairs. After a period of refit, modernization, and training, *Pennsylvania* rejoined the Pacific Fleet on April 23, 1943. NH 64475

Tennessee

Tennessee floats next to sunken *West Virginia* at Battleship Row's Berth F-6 alongside Ford Island. The battleships are seen from on top of *Oklahoma*'s overturned hull. *Tennessee* was pinned between the anchor points of Berth F-6 and *West Virginia* and held fast. The forward mooring quay of F-6 was removed using explosives, freeing *Tennessee* to move to the Navy Yard for repairs. NH 50770

Japanese bombs struck the roofs of *Tennessee*'s Turrets Two and Three. This view shows the hole in the top of Turret Three. *Tennessee* was repaired and ready for service by December 20, 1941. NH 64479

Honolulu

Light cruiser *Honolulu* was docked at the Navy Yard and heavily damaged by a near-miss. A 250-kilogram (551 pound) bomb passed through the pier and exploded in the water below twenty feet from the hull amidships. The concussive force of the explosion was magnified by the shallow water and the shore. This opened hull plates below the armor belt causing heavy flooding. NH 64478 / NH 83060

Raleigh

Berthed on the west side of Ford Island at Berth F-12, *Raleigh* was struck by a torpedo at 8 a.m., minutes after the attack began. The light cruiser's forward engine room and both forward boiler rooms were immediately flooded. Sailors began jettisoning weight on the port side of the ship and although counter-flooding was attempted, it did not correct the cruiser's list. A barge was tied alongside and kept *Raleigh* afloat. Capsized *Utah* can be seen at right behind the tug. NH 50769

During the second wave of the attack, a Japanese dive bomber sent a bomb into *Raleigh*'s main deck around frame 112—a point about two-thirds the length of the ship. It passed through three decks and exited into the harbor before exploding. This opened more hull plates that contributed to flooding below decks. 80-G-32448

Shaw

The forward magazine of destroyer *Shaw* explodes providing one of the most iconic photos of the Japanese attack on Pearl Harbor. Sitting high above the water in floating dry dock *YFD-2*, *Shaw* made an excellent target for three Val dive-bombers that put 250-kilogram bombs into the destroyer, the last of which opened the ship's fuel oil tanks. Heat from the burning fuel cooked off the ammunition in the forward magazine, blowing off *Shaw*'s bow. NARA

As *Shaw* began to burn, *YFD-2* was flooded in an attempt to limit the damage to the dock. However, shrapnel from the explosion of *Shaw*'s forward magazine and the fires, coupled with five near-misses by bombs, holed its hull. *YFD-2* is seen sitting on the bottom at a fifteen-degree list to port, with *Shaw* burning inside. The smoke stack of tug *Sotoyomo*, which was inside *YFD-2* ahead of *Shaw*, can be seen between the two uprights of *YFD-2*. *Sotoyomo* was heavily damaged by fire and shrapnel from *Shaw*, but was eventually rebuilt and returned to the fleet. NARA

Looking into *YFD-2* from the bow of the dry dock shows *Shaw*'s bow sitting awkwardly to starboard while the rest of the ship sits upright. The explosion and fire have melted the destroyer's superstructure. The top rail of the port side of the dry dock is completely submerged, foreground, with the exception of the handrail. The heavily damaged and listing *California* can be seen in the background to the right. NARA

By December 8, *YFD-2* has been counter-flooded, leveling it below the surface. *Shaw* has become buoyant and has moved to the stern of the dry dock while the top of the tug *Sotoyomo* peeks up from behind the catwalk in the center. Seaplane tender *Curtiss* is seen at left and Battleship Row is in the center background. NH 50771

Sailors begin the task of securing *Shaw* before the dry dock is floated. Men can be seen on most of the decks, including the superstructure. A motor launch from the destroyer tender *Dobbin* (AD-3) is alongside. 80-G-32618

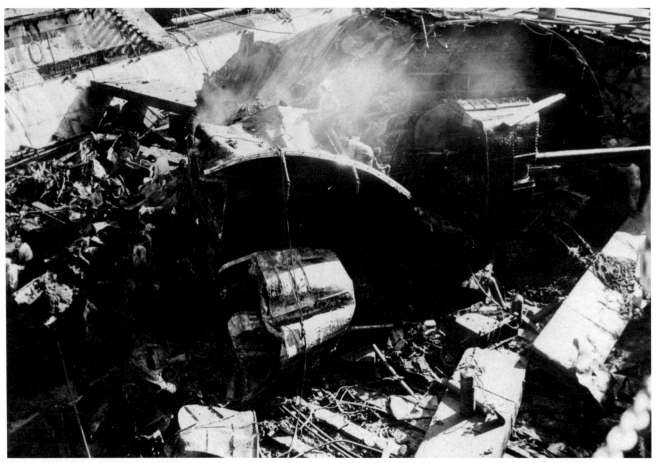

One month after the attack the salvage operation was underway. *YFD-2* was raised and the bow of *Shaw* is seen on January 11, 1942. When the destroyer's forward magazine, located aft of the forward 5-inch/38-caliber gun turrets, exploded, it severed the bow from the rest of the ship. NH 84000

Workers at the Pearl Harbor Navy Yard fashioned a new bow and foremast for *Shaw* to enable the destroyer to sail 3,630 miles across the Pacific Ocean to the Mare Island Navy Yard, north of San Francisco. Note that much of the destroyer's armament, including a trio of quintuple 21-inch torpedo launchers as well as its after 5-inch/38-caliber guns, have been removed. NH 50005

Shaw is seen after its arrival at Mare Island with fire damage to its hull visible along the waterline. The submarine under construction on the way to the left is *Whale* (SS-239). NH 43530

The Mare Island Naval Shipyard built a new bow for *Shaw* and the destroyer is seen at right in the yard's dry dock. The new bow, surrounded by scaffolding, was mated to the after section of the destroyer during the late spring and early summer of 1942. While being rebuilt, the destroyer was modernized with a Mk 33 fire control, a pair of Mk 51 gun directors, two twin-mount 40mm cannon and six 20mm anti-aircraft guns. *Shaw* returned to the fleet at the end of August 1942. 80-G-21336

View of *YFD-2* showing what the floating dry dock looked like when surfaced. This photo was taken as the dry dock arrived at the Pearl Harbor Navy Yard on August 23, 1940. Destroyer *Shaw* made a highly visible target sitting inside the dock. 80-G-411134

Curtiss

View from the stern of *Curtiss* looking into the hangar showing the damage caused when a bomb exploded inside the ship on the main deck. The hangar doors were destroyed along with Vought OS2U Kingfisher (Buno. 2199), which burned on deck. NARA 19-N-26297

Reverse angle view of the hangar deck shortly after the fires were extinguished. Note the starboard crane that was impacted by a Japanese Val dive-bomber as well as the burned-out OS2U Kingfisher. Firefighting gear is strewn about the deck.

NARA 19-N-26301

A Val dive-bomber from the carrier *Akagi* that was struck by anti-aircraft fire careened into *Curtiss*, impacting the ship's forward crane, located on the starboard side boat deck. The Val burned on the boat deck while three more bombs were dropped on or near the ship by Japanese dive-bombers. NARA 19-N-26295

Looking at the forward end of the hangar bay on the main deck of *Curtiss* showing the damage caused by the explosion of a 250-kilogram bomb. The bomb entered the ship three decks above and exploded here at the entrance to the battery shop. During the attack, nineteen were killed and many wounded on board *Curtiss*. NARA 19-N-26296

Vestal

When *Arizona*'s forward magazine exploded, fuel oil on the surface of the harbor caught fire, which in turn began to burn the hull of the repair ship *Vestal*. The explosion blew *Vestal*'s commanding officer, Cmdr. Cassin Young, overboard and subsequently someone gave the order to abandon ship. Young swam back to *Vestal*, countermanded the order and, cutting the lines at 8:45 a.m., got the ship moving away from *Arizona*. With the help of a tug, *Vestal* moved to McGrew's Point within the harbor. She was taking on water and Cmdr. Young decided to beach the ship on Aiea Shoal. NH 64480

Cassin and *Downes*

Late in the afternoon of December 7, a photographer captured the aftermath of the Japanese attack in Dry Dock Number One. *Downes* is upright at left, with *Cassin* rolled 30 degrees to starboard resting on its sister ship. Battleship *Pennsylvania* is seen behind the destroyers. Note the large amount of fuel oil on the surface of the dry dock, which was flooded to limit damage and keep the ships' magazines cool. NH 64482

Stern-view of destroyer *Cassin*, with *Downes* at right. Shrapnel damage ruptured the fuel oil tanks of both destroyers and the oil was, in turn, ignited by bombs dropped in or near the dry dock. Heat from the burning fuel oil did cook off a number of torpedoes, depth charges, and 5-inch ammunition in ready lockers on deck. Although attacking Japanese planes focused their attention on Navy ships in the harbor, they left the majority of the Navy Yard undamaged as evidenced by the large warehouse and the yard cranes in the background that appear unscathed. 80-G-32431

Once the dry dock was drained, fire damage to the hull of *Downes* could be assessed. The hull was twisted and wrinkled, damaged by fire, shrapnel, and the weight of *Cassin* crashing down on her before the dry dock was flooded. NH 54556

Looking at the forward, starboard side of *Downes*, showing fire damage and the destruction of the superstructure. The destroyer's pilothouse was completely destroyed. The second shop building, above right, suffered some fire damage, but the majority of the Navy Yard infrastructure was untouched. Many of the damaged ships were quickly returned to service because the Naval Yard was virtually untouched during the attack. NH 54561

Salvage operations saved the majority of *Downes*'s internal machinery and equipment. These parts were shipped to Mare Island where they were incorporated into a new hull and re-commissioned, again as DD-375, on November 15, 1943. She returned to the fleet on March 8, 1944, and saw service at Wotje Atoll, Eniwetok, Saipan, Tinian, the Battle for Leyte Gulf, and Iwo Jima. NH 54558

Cassin is seen in Dry Dock Number One on January 23, 1941, undergoing salvage. She still rests against *Downes*, but both ships have been secured. *Cassin*'s propellers and after armament have already been removed. NH 55061

Views of Dry Dock Number One showing the cruiser *Raleigh* undergoing repairs while *Downes* and *Cassin* are being salvaged, February 5, 1942. Sailors man the rails as the water level in the dock is drained.

NH 54562

NH 54564

What was left of *Downes*'s hull was refloated and tugged out of Dry Dock Number One. This hulk was scrapped while the guts of *Downes* were rebuilt at Mare Island Naval Shipyard in California. NH 54557

Cassin was removed from Dry Dock Number One on February 18, 1942, and prepared for the long tow to the Mare Island Naval Shipyard, north of San Francisco. Here she was rebuilt and modernized, rejoining the fleet on April 22, 1944. NH 55063

Nevada

Aerial view of *Nevada* aground on Waipio Peninsula in the Ford Island Channel in the days after the Japanese attack. The battleship is attended to by a number of repair ships and tugs and is still leaking fuel oil at this point. NARA

This massive patch was engineered and built by the Pearl Harbor Navy Yard to seal a large hole in *Oklahoma*. Because *Oklahoma* was not ready for salvage, divers tried to fit the patch to the damaged area of *Nevada*'s hull. After installation, the patch would not maintain a watertight seal and had to be removed. The crane barge *Gaylord*, from the Hawaiian Dredging Co., is seen manipulating the patch into place.

NH 64476

NH 45463

NH 45464

NH 45465

Pearl Harbor Navy Yard workers assemble a patch to cover a bomb hole in *Nevada*'s port bow. NH 64485

The explosion of a bomb below decks distorted the *Nevada*'s main deck forward of the Number One Turret. NH 64484

Anchored at Waipio Peninsula looking aft from the bow shows the distortion of *Nevada*'s main deck from the torpedo and bomb explosions below. Three-gun Number One Turret and two-gun Number Two Turret hold 14-inch/45-caliber guns. These batteries were supplemented by twenty-one 5-inch/51 caliber guns and a pair of 3-inch/50-caliber anti-aircraft cannon. NARA

On February 18, 1942, *Nevada* was escorted from its resting point in the waters off Waipio Peninsula to Dry Dock Number Two for repairs. Ford Island's Hangar Number Six is visible in the background at left. Of the tugs visible, *Osceola* (YT-129) is identifiable at right assisting *Nevada* across the harbor. NARA

Once in dry dock, the patch on the port bow shows its location at Frame 7. The bomb's exit hole at the complex curve of the turn of the bilge made designing and installing the patch under water a difficult task. NH 64494

Torpedo damage in *Nevada*'s port-side hull at Frame 41, fourteen feet above the keel, was revealed to onlookers after the patch was removed in dry dock. NARA

Seawater streams from a split-seam in *Nevada*'s starboard hull. Dished-in hull area just above the bilge was most likely caused by a near-miss bomb explosion. NARA

As evidenced by this view of *Nevada*'s hull, had she sailed out of the harbor in pursuit of the Japanese, she would not have made it very far and would have, most likely, ended up on the bottom of the Pacific Ocean. Torpedo impact and explosion damage is seen on the vertical surfaces with large splits in the hull seams on the horizontal hull plates. NARA

California

In the hours after the air raid, a small armada of ships came to the aid of *California*, attempting to keep the battleship afloat. Smoke from fires on *West Virginia* obscures the background. The mooring quays for Berth F-3 can be seen holding *California* fast as she lists to port. Having absorbed a pair of torpedo hits and a single bomb strike, the battleship listed as far as sixteen degrees to port before counter-flooding nearly righted her. It took three days, but *California* eventually settled to the harbor bottom. NH 64474

Assisting at *California*'s stern is the minesweeper *Bobolink* (AM-20, left), with minesweeper *Vireo* and water barge *YW-10* at right. The battleship's main deck is awash as she settles to the harbor bottom. NH 95569

In February 1942, *California*'s basket main mast was removed to help lighten the ship before refloating her. The base of the mast was cut, then lifted by a floating crane.

NH 55037

2/13/42
F.C.P. U.S.S. Cal
MAINMAST,
CUT, AWA

NH 55035

Bow view of *California* as unwatering progresses, seen on March 30, 1942. At this point she had been afloat for seven days. Note the wooden cofferdam attached to the forward section of the ship and the lack of guns in the forward turrets. The battleship entered Dry Dock Number Two on April 9, 1942. NH 55036

As the dry dock is emptied, the mud lines can be seen on the hull of *California*. The guns were removed from all but Turret Number Four. The main deck stern is littered with sandbags used to reinforce the cofferdam during the trip from Berth F-3 to the dry dock. NH 64483

The second torpedo to strike *California* hit between Frames 99 and 104, penetrating the hull below the armor belt. The blast from the torpedo's explosion buckled a number of interior bulkheads. 80-G-32917

Rebuilding *California* and getting her ready to fight. Here the battleship is seen on July 18, 1942, as one of her 14-inch/50-caliber main guns is reinstalled in Turret Number One. Guns have been installed in Turrets Three and Four; however, their armored tops have not yet been fitted. *California* received the attention of workers at the Pearl Harbor Navy Yard until October 1942, when she sailed to the Puget Sound Naval Shipyard to complete her modernization. In June 1944, *California* was back in action supporting the shore bombardment of Saipan. NH 83997

West Virginia, June 1942

As *West Virginia* burns, with *Tennessee* in the background, a sailor is rescued from the water. Burning fuel oil can be seen in the background surrounding the hull of *West Virginia*. 80-G-19930

Minesweeper *Tern* (AM-31) fights fires on *West Virginia* while its gun crew keeps a watchful eye on the sky for another wave of Japanese aircraft. The silhouette of *Tennessee* can be seen behind *West Virginia*'s Turret Number One. NH 64477

A Japanese 15-inch artillery shell converted into an aerial bomb is seen lodged inside *West Virginia* on the second deck, port side, near Frame 63. Two of these 1,750-pound bombs were dropped on the battleship, but neither exploded. Experts believe as many as seven torpedoes struck the ship, with one or two entering through the holes of previous strikes. NH 64305

Pearl Harbor Navy Yard workers built this massive batch to fit under the ship's armor belt to enable the unwatering process to begin. Underwater concrete was used extensively to seal the sides and bottom of the patches. NH 64489

Six months and one day after the Japanese attack, *West Virginia* was towed across the harbor to Dry Dock Number One on June 8, 1942. Note the hull patches amid ships below the 10-inch dewatering pipes. NH 64491

Bow-on view of *West Virginia* in Dry Dock Number One clearly shows the armor belt and hull patches. The Navy Yard's cranes, untouched during the attack, quickly went to work repairing damaged ships.

80-G-13154

Work progresses on *West Virginia*, seen on June 17, 1942. Many of the damaged areas have been cut from the superstructure. Once seaworthy, the battleship was sailed to the Puget Sound Naval Shipyard for restoration and modernization. NH 83507

Graphic illustration of the damage caused below the waterline by Japanese aerial torpedoes. Sections of the hull patches have been removed and the concrete used to seal them can be seen at the base of the remaining patch. NH 83508

Oglala, July 1942

Two days after the attack, minelayer *Oglala* rests on her side at 1010 Dock. This view is looking from *Oglala*'s bow to stern. The devastation along Battleship Row can be seen in the distance. The minelayer's 375-foot long hull was penetrated between Frames 68 and 86 with inrushing water flooding the fireroom and the engine room. NH 60672

Salvage operations are underway on *Oglala* with a diver in the water near the motor launch at right. Divers made 542 dives, spending more than 2,000 hours underwater, cutting off 150 tons of weight from the ship's upper structure to lighten her and improve the minelayer's stability once afloat. NH 60673

On April 11, 1942, the first attempt to raise *Oglala* failed when salvage pontoons broke free of their mounts. The second attempt, which was successful, brought *Oglala* to the surface on April 23. *Oklahoma* and *West Virginia* are seen in the background. NH44580

Damage to *Oglala* occurred when a torpedo passed under her hull and struck the light cruiser *Helena*. Concussion from the torpedo's explosion caved in *Oglala*'s hull, flooding her interior. Because of her early design, watertight compartments were lacking and the weight of the inrushing seawater caused the minelayer to roll over. NH 84007

Oglala out of dry dock and ready to depart for the West Coast. The shop building behind the dock has been given a coat of camouflage paint. NH 64236

After repair at the Navy Yard, *Oglala* was ready to sail to the West Coast for modernization. She was converted to an internal combustion engine repair ship and designated ARG-1. She supported various patrol and landing craft in waters surrounding New Guinea and the Philippines. NH 61896

Arizona

Navajo (AT-64) and *Tern* (AM-31) spray water onto *Arizona* two days after the attack to cool the ship, still glowing red hot after its forward magazine exploded and the vessel burned. Through the battle and the subsequent fire, the canvas awning over the battleship's stern is still in place and is seen forward of the stern crane. NH 83064

The mooring quays for Berth F-7 can be seen alongside *Arizona* on December 9, 1941. The battleship's fires are out and damage can be assessed. Turret Number One is completely submerged having ridden the collapsed decks down after the forward magazine exploded. Turret Number Two is barely above water, and the fire-blackened foremast has collapsed. Men can be seen on the searchlight platform of the after mast. NARA

Arizona's mangled bow protrudes from below the harbor's surface. Burning fuel oil from *Arizona* drifted toward *West Virginia*, engulfing the stern of the battleship. This view shows how close the ships were moored to each other along Battleship Row. NARA

Pearl Harbor Navy Yard Diving Launch Number Seven sits off *Arizona*'s starboard side with a diver underwater near the starboard rail. Notice how the mid-ship's deck house has collapsed forward as a result of the loss of supporting structure as the decks below disappeared when the forward magazine exploded. The diving platform, forward of Turret Number Two, rides at anchor in the space usually occupied by Turret Number One. NARA

Close-up of the damage done to the foremast and mid-ships section of the battleship. Even the plates surrounding the armored bridge were warped from the explosion and subsequent fire. The large structure above and to the left is one of the Navy Yard's floating cranes. NARA

Arizona's foremast is removed by the Navy Yard's floating crane. NARA

On February 25, 1942, the guns from Turret Number Three had been salvaged while the last cannon in Turret Number Four will soon be lifted out. These guns were set aside to protect the island of Oahu, three for Battery Arizona and three for Battery Pennsylvania, sited at Kahe Point Military Reservation, in the hills west of Pearl Harbor. NARA

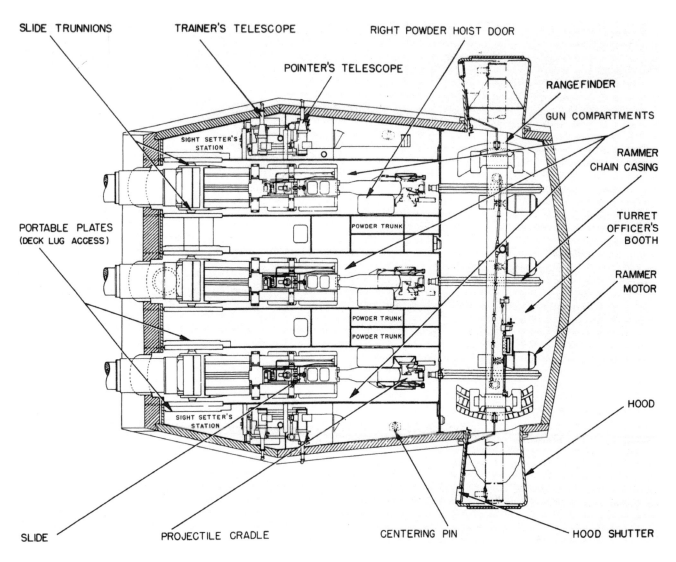

SLIDE TRUNNIONS

TRAINER'S TELESCOPE

RIGHT POWDER HOIST DOOR

POINTER'S TELESCOPE

RANGEFINDER

GUN COMPARTMENTS

RAMMER CHAIN CASING

SIGHT SETTER'S STATION

POWDER TRUNK

PORTABLE PLATES (DECK LUG ACCESS)

TURRET OFFICER'S BOOTH

RAMMER MOTOR

POWDER TRUNK

POWDER TRUNK

SIGHT SETTER'S STATION

HOOD

SLIDE

PROJECTILE CRADLE

CENTERING PIN

HOOD SHUTTER

Interior drawing of a large caliber triple gun turret as installed on U.S. Navy battleships of the day. U.S. NAVY

By June 1942, the majority of *Arizona*'s forward structure has been removed and the guns of Turrets Three and Four have been salvaged. NARA

A diver, covered in fuel oil, emerges from below decks of Turret Number Three during the ammunition and powder recovery process. Air was pumped below decks to minimize the explosion hazard but workers were still required to wear respirators or have an external air supply when inside the ship. NARA

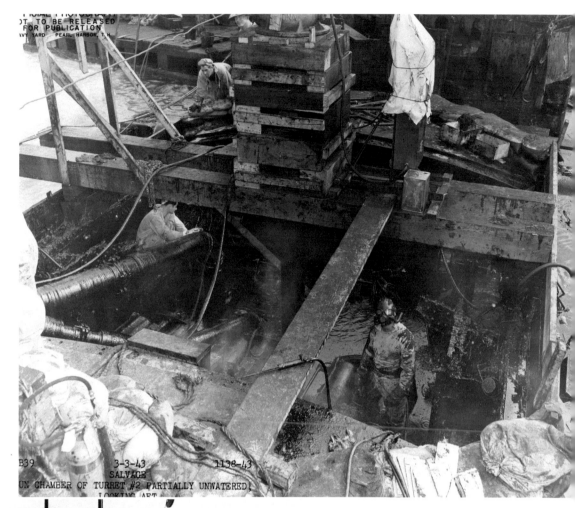

The top of Turret Number Two has been removed and men are seen unwatering the space. The turret assembly went more than fifty feet down into the ship where the shell and powder handing rooms were located. NARA

Using the Navy Yard's large, floating crane, salvors prepare to remove the center 14-inch/45-caliber gun from *Arizona*'s Turret Number Two. Temporary walkways, some floating and some attached to the ship, have been installed to make work life easier for the men. *Oklahoma* can be seen in the center left, having been rolled level and is having its upper deck structure removed to lighten the ship. The hulk tied to Berth F-6 alongside Ford Island, where *Tennessee* was moored during the attack, is *YF-331*, ex-USS *Intrepid*, a steel-hulled, three-mast Bark used as a training ship. She was decommissioned in December 1921, and sold for use as a barge. Shortly after the Pearl Harbor attack, she was reacquired by the Navy to serve as a sludge removal barge.

NARA

The center gun from Turret Number Two is lifted from the wreckage. The gun barrel is covered in mud and marine life. Although the breech was covered in mud and fuel oil, it was operable by hand. NARA

After the barrels were removed from each of the turrets, the gun slides were lifted away. This is the gun slide for Turret Number Two. NARA

The Navy Yard's floating crane begins to lift the armored, rotating section of the turret from position number three. The forward section of *Arizona*'s upper decks along with both masts and the superstructure have been removed by the time of this photo, April 19, 1943. NARA

Removing the internal components of Turret Number Three from *Arizona* and setting it on the deck of the floating crane. NARA

The yard's 150-ton floating crane lifts the turret housing from Turret Number Three on April 19, 1943. NARA

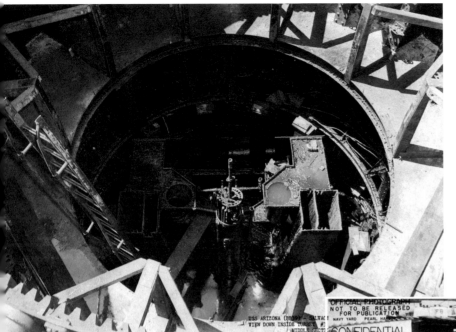

With the rotation portion of the turret assembly removed, this photo shows the interior of the turret with its ammunition hosting mechanisms. Water can be seen four decks down inside the barbette. NARA

Interior of Turret Number Three after removing the armored, rotating section of the turret assembly. Torpedo nets have been installed to protect the battleship moored behind *Arizona*. NARA

The ammunition lifts from inside Turret Number Three are raised clear of the barbette, completing the removal of this section. Compare the size of the turret's internal workings with the crane's door, a little larger than a six-foot-tall man, below at right in this photo. NARA

Turret Number Four received the salvor's attention in February 1942. The center gun was removed from the slide and held for installation at one of two coastal defense batteries overlooking Pearl Harbor. NARA

With the guns gone, the side armor plate from Turret Number Four was removed next. Note the elevated walkways from the mooring quay over and across the ship. NARA

Once Turret Number Four was empty, a cofferdam was installed around the barbette to aid in unwatering the below deck spaces. NARA

Workers prepare Turret Number Four's lower section, the part of the turret holding the shell and powder elevators, for removal from the ship. The internal assemblies of the turrets had to be removed before the battleship's 14-inch shells could be recovered. NARA

BUOY AT
BOW

TURRET
#2

SUPERSTRUTURE
DECK

BARBETTE
#3

COFFERDAM AROUND
BARBETTE #4

COFFERDAM
AT STERN

FRAME 78

Aerial view of the *Arizona*'s salvage operation showing the thoroughness of the removal of the ship's upper structure. The size of the mooring quays is seen to good advantage in this view. Each quay is built upon thirty-five concrete pilings and is approximately forty feet in length. NARA

Oklahoma

Oklahoma's capsized hull at rest after the attack and the rescue effort to free men trapped within the hull. This stern view shows the starboard bilge keel facing upward at 90 degrees. 80-G-32453

Looking bow-on at a cardboard model of *Oklahoma* built to show divers and other salvage experts the position of the ship, the depth of the water, and the large amount of the ship's superstructure and masts that were buried in the harbor's mud. This model helped many comprehend the extent of the damage and give a visual reference to the part of the hull above water. NARA

Side view of the *Oklahoma* model showing the water line, mud line, and sections of the ship buried at the bottom of the harbor. NARA

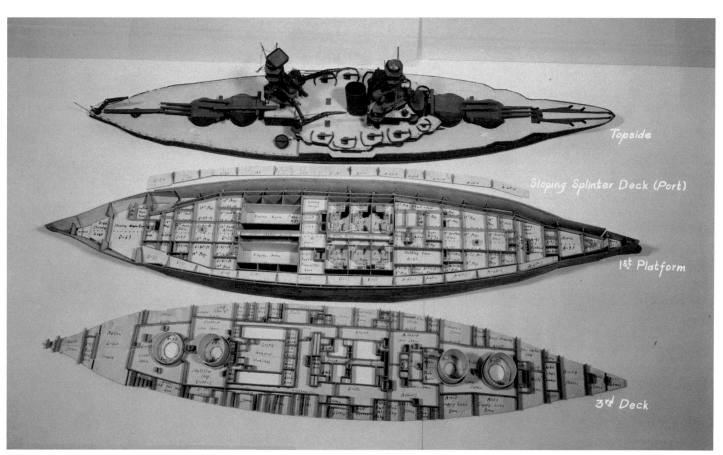

The *Oklahoma* salvage model was also used to help divers familiarize themselves with the ship's internal compartments. For divers, these compartments would be inverted when they entered the ship to seal passageways and holes in the hull to help create an air bubble inside, as well as when they were removing mud and sludge to lighten the ship before it was rolled level prior to refloating. NARA

More than fifteen holes were cut into *Oklahoma*'s hull to gain access to the ship's starboard side oil bunkers. Approximately 350,000 gallons of fuel oil were removed to help lighten the ship. She had topped off her tanks just a few days prior to the attack and had more than one million gallons of fuel oil on board when she rolled over. Removal of the remaining oil would have to wait until the ship was righted as access to the port side tanks were restricted due to the battleship's position in the mud. NARA

Oklahoma's propellers were dismantled on the sunken battleship, then lifted onto waiting barges for removal. The Navy Yard dive boat is seen at left with sailors attending to a diver under water, while one of the mud-encrusted propeller blades can be seen on the deck of the barge at right, just behind the sailor crouching on deck. The starboard propeller has been removed and the shaft can be seen above water at right. NARA

To prepare for the righting operation, engineers built and tested a series of models to obtain predictions on how the battleship hulk would behave as it rolled upright. A section of *Oklahoma*'s hull was modeled to determine where to attach the righting bents and to confirm estimates of the amount of force needed to roll the hull. NARA

U.S.S. OKLAHOMA-SALVAGE   12/19/42   5459-42
1/16 SCALE MODEL FOR ROLLING TEST IN ABOUT
140° POSITION.

NARA

Engineers from the Pacific Bridge Company of San Francisco also built a one-sixteenth scale model to test how the harbor bottom mud would react to the moving forces of *Oklahoma*'s hull. The model is seen in the rolling pit with its top over 140 degrees to port. In addition the battleship's dead weight, a sizeable mud wave built up in front of *Oklahoma*'s hull as she rolled. The resistance of the harbor bottom mud required greater pulling force to roll the battleship's hull.

OFFICIAL PHOTOGRAPH
NOT TO BE RELEASED
FOR PUBLICATION
NAVY YARD   PEARL HARBOR, T.H.

U.S.S. OKLAHOMA-SALVAGE   12/19/42   5458-42
1/16 SCALE ROLLING MODEL - MUD WAVE IN FRONT
AT ABOUT 135° POSITION.

NARA

Preparing the Winches

Engineers placed twenty-one electric winches set on concrete anchors along the Ford Island shoreline. Using a block system, each winch was capable of a 20-ton pull. NARA

Two anchor rod assemblies seen after delivery and before installation. The two units are stacked one on top of the other. These were embedded in concrete to hold the block cables.

NARA

NARA

Righting operations were begun on March 8, 1943, and this view shows the pulling cables stretched from the ship to Ford Island one week later. Cables passed through a block system, which increased their pull by a factor of seventeen. The cables then stretched from shore to the top of the righting bents, then passed down to the hull of the ship where they split into four leads that were attached to lugs at the frame stations. The starboard fuel oil tanks were pumped full of air, lightening the hull by almost 20,000 pounds. NARA

Rolling

Once all of the hardware was in position, righting of *Oklahoma* began on March 8, 1943. The ship is seen here as tension is taken up on the cables.

NARA

USS OKLAHOMA (BB37) – SALVAGE   3-8-43   1346-43
VIEW UNDER RIGHTING TACKLES LOOKING FORWARD, SHIP IN 130° POSITION

NARA

Connection points for the three-inch cables that stretched from the blocks to the tops of the righting bents. This view looks toward the hulk of *Arizona* above left and shows pendants 19, 20, and 21 (each line matching a winch on Ford Island). NARA

Eleven days after the righting operation began, on March 19, 1943, *Oklahoma* sits in the 90-degree position. The barge with the tall smoke stack is *IX-56* (the former fleet tug *Navajo* AT-52). *IX-56* had been stricken from the Naval Register on April 24, 1937, but was re-commissioned as a miscellaneous vessel on March 15, 1942, because the Navy needed additional deck space on the harbor during the fleet salvage operation. The tugboat was tied up alongside the hulk of *Oklahoma* for the duration of the recovery effort and served as a floating messing facility. NARA

The rolling operation continued with *Oklahoma* passing through 85 degrees later in the day of March 19, 1943. The ship's name is visible below the stern rail. NARA

Once the hull rotated to the 70-degree position, the wooden righting bents were removed and the pulling continued directly from lugs attached to the ship's frame stations. This view looks from Ford Island into the harbor with *Oklahoma* having rolled to the 68-degree position. NARA

ASBF (V-J-1) #21700 - 3/21/43
USS OKLAHOMA (BB37) - Salvage

By March 21, 1943, the battleship had been rolled to the 40-degree upright position. NARA

On board *Oklahoma* at the 40-degree position a sailor climbs over the Number One Turret. The deck is covered with mud and oil, and the majority of the superstructure had been cut away prior to the righting effort. NARA

ASBF(V-J-1) #21728 - 3/26/43
U.S.S. OKLAHOMA - Salvage -
Looking aft from about frame

Standing on deck at Frame 95, the large amount of damage that occurred when the battleship capsized and the subsequent stripping of the hull is evident. *Oklahoma* was too badly damaged to rebuild. NARA

The forward half of *Oklahoma* is viewed from Ford Island showing the battleship at the 17-degree position on April 7, 1943, almost one day to the month when righting operations began. A floating walkway was built to enable workers to pass from the battleship's hull to *IX-56* for meals, then back to Ford Island. NARA

View of *Oklahoma* from the harbor side looking toward Ford Island showing the damage to the mid-ships structure, April 7. The armored bridge is visible behind Turret Number Two in the center of the photo. NARA

Once at the 10-degree position, the deck was almost walkable, and work began in earnest to prepare the ship to be floated. Anchor chain is being craned from the deck as water continues to be pumped over the side. NARA

An oversized clinometer was installed on one of the after deck house walls to give workers a visible clue as to the ship's position. The sailor is checking the position as the ship sits listing 10-degrees to port. NARA

ASPF(V-J-1) #22161 - 5/16/43
USS OKLAHOMA - Salvage -
Clinometer with ship in about
10° position

On June 18, 1943, *Oklahoma* was photographed listing at 2 degrees, 10 minutes, and is held fast to the shore with the righting cables wrapped around the turret barbettes. Holding her in this position prevented the battleship from slipping into the hole carved when the hull was rotated upright. Two additional walkways have been added to enable workers to access the center and aft sections of the ship. NARA

NASPH 11 147 - 18 June, 1943.
U.S.S. OKLAHOMA (BB37) SALVAGE
Aerial view from starboard bow
in 2°-10' position.

Workers at the Pearl Harbor Navy Yard built a five-part patch to cover damage on the ship's port side from Frames 43 to 75—130 feet long and 57.5 feet high. The patch has a steel framework with a wooden face that is placed next to the damaged hull and sealed with concrete. Other smaller patches were installed, including sections covering the areas between Frames 31 and 43 as well as Frames 74 and 96. This is the forward-most section of the patch showing the front edge of the patch and how it aligns with the damaged hull. NARA

The Navy Yard's 150-ton floating crane rotates the second section of the five-part hull patch. The supporting truss work is shown behind the wooden facing. NARA

This section of the hull patch covered Frames 50-56. Note how workers have rigged a walkway using a steel I-beam suspended by cables over the top of the patch. NARA

After divers used hook bolts to secure the patch to the side of the hull, underwater concrete was poured inside to form a watertight seal. Here workers use the Tremie placement method to pour batches of concrete into the patch. The Tremie method keeps the lower end of the pipe in concrete and as more concrete is poured in, gravity forces the concrete into the form, displacing the water above the concrete without washing it out. More than 1,000 tons of concrete were used to seal the hull patches. NARA

During the salvage operation, both Navy and Pacific Bridge Company divers worked inside *Oklahoma*'s hull to remove mud, seal various outlets through the hull, and make the interior watertight. The balance of the fuel oil was removed along with the bodies of 400 men who lost their lives on board *Oklahoma* during the attack. Here a Pacific Bridge Company diver ascends a ladder to the diving platform after inspecting the five-part main patch. NARA

Seaman First Class Harriman has his hard hat diving helmet removed after working inside the hull of *Oklahoma* on November 12, 1943. Fuel oil floating inside the ship continues to coat everything at this point in the salvage effort. NARA

More than two years after
the Japanese attack,
on December 28, 1943,
Oklahoma was eased into
Dry Dock Number Two.
The ship listed to starboard
almost three degrees in an
effort to reduce the pressure
on the five-part hull patch on
the port side. NARA

OFFICIAL USN PHOTO
NAVY YARD, PEARL HARBOR
CONFIDENTIAL

USS OKLAHOMA (BB37) – SALVAGE   12-29-43   7006-43
VIEW LOOKING AFT ON PORT SIDE FROM ABOUT FRAME 35 AFTER LANDING
IN DRYDOCK

The following day, Dry Number Two was drained to begin the task of making the battleship watertight and to salvage the ship's guns
and auxiliary machinery. Rather than use counter-flooding to correct *Oklahoma*'s list during the harbor crossing and dry-docking, four
submersible salvage pontoons, each with a lifting capacity of 80 tons, were attached to the hull patch. A wooden cofferdam can be seen
lining the stern rail of the ship—similar to the type used on *Arizona*'s Turret Number Four, *California*, and *Oglala*—from Frame 85 to Frame
115 behind the massive hull patch. This was done to increase the waterplane area and improve stability during the refloating operation. NARA

Divers installed lines to keep the rudder centered during the tow across the harbor. They can be seen stretching from the rudder to the upper sections of the port and starboard hull. NARA

Standing near the stern and looking forward at the hull damage, the amount of distortion below the waterline can be seen. Compare the size of the workers at left with the size of the patch and how the lower sections of the patch's end conform to the damaged hull. NARA

At a point 128 feet from the bow, between Frames 32 and 44, hull plates have been blown in and decks distorted from exploding Japanese torpedoes. NARA

OFFICIAL U.S.N. PHOTO
NAVY YARD, PEARL HARBOR
CONFIDENTIAL

USS OKLAHOMA (BB37) - SALVAGE   12-31-43   7122-43
LKG FWD ON PORT SIDE FROM ABOUT FR 77 DURING REMOVAL OF MAIN PATCH

Once the five-part patch was removed, the full extent of the hull damage could be seen. The armor belt is distorted and completely missing over a large area. Note the shipyard worker standing on the concrete at the bottom of the patch. He gives scale to the amount of concrete used just to seal this one patch. NARA

Utah

Gunnery training ship *Utah* was moored at Berth F-11 on the western side of Ford Island, typically reserved for aircraft carriers. As the colors were hoisted, a torpedo struck the bow of the ship and she began to list immediately. At 8:12 a.m., she rolled 165 degrees, capsizing at her moorings. Tapping was heard on the hull and after obtaining a cutting torch from nearby *Raleigh*, ten men were rescued from the bottom of the ship. In total, *Utah* took six officers and fifty-eight men with her. By early 1943, there was a plan afoot to roll *Utah* upright and raise her using the same methods as those that refloated *Oklahoma*. The salvage effort is seen in the opening stages on June 3, 1943. The hulk tied to *Utah* in front of the barge is *YF-331* (ex-USS *Intrepid*). NARA

NARA

Six months later, in November 1943, the uprights for the parbuckling operation to right *Utah* have been installed on the former battleship's overturned hull. Fuel oil flows from the hulk moving south with the current. Torpedo nets have been installed to protect Berth F-10 from future attacks.

NARA

USS UTAH (AG16) – SALVAGE 2-1-44 809-44
VIEW FROM SHORE SHOWING METHOD OF OUTHAULING RIGHTING TACKLE FOR
CONNECTION TO PENDANTS FROM SHIP

Winches for righting *Utah* have been installed on the western side of Ford Island and the cables strung from ship to shore. They have yet to be connected to the winches in this February 1, 1944, photograph. The large number of ships tied together in nests can be seen in Middle Loch. NARA

By February 10, 1944, *Utah* had been rotated through 90 degrees and the righting bents had reached their useful limit. NARA

After the righting bents had rotated the ship to 90 degrees, the blister plates were removed to enable new hitch pads to be attached to the hull. Eventually the list was reduced to 38 degrees, but during the pull *Utah* slid toward Ford Island, rather than rotate upright, and the salvage attempt was abandoned. NARA

YARD TUGS AT WORK

The unsung heroes in the immediate aftermath of the air raid were the sailors on board the Yard Craft working inside the harbor. Garbage lighter and tug duty is very necessary, but unglamorous at best. However, it was these men that sprang into action to move vessels, rescue men, and assist in fighting the massive shipboard conflagration around the harbor.

Garbage lighter *YG-17* was alongside the battleship *Nevada* when the Japanese planes began their attack. *YG-17* was not needed by the Silver State's battlewagon and went to fight fires on *Arizona, Tennessee*, and *West Virginia*. *YG-21* was at the south end of battleship row and fought fires on board *California* until 12:30 p.m. When no longer needed at *California*, *YG-21* spent the next five and a half hours fighting fires on board *West Virginia*. *YT-129* was also dispatched to aid *California* in fighting fires, and the tug's pumps were used to flood the battleship's after magazines to prevent an explosion.

Tug *YT-130* assisted in getting several ships underway, while *YT-152* aided the cruiser *Phoenix* and the ammunition ship *Pyro* (AE-1) into the harbor channel.

YT-142 went to fight fires on *Arizona* and rescued a number of men from the oil-soaked water around the ship. When officers on board *Arizona* told the tug's captain that the battleship was beyond saving, *YT-142* plucked more men from the water and took them across the harbor to 1010 Dock. From here, *YT-142* crossed the harbor to fight fires on *California* and after the air raid helped with salvage work and eventual refloating of the battleship.

Early in the attack, *YT-146* moved the repair ship *Vestal* away from *Arizona* and beached her near Aiea.

She then went to move *Oglala* away from the cruiser *Helena*. After fighting fires on *Nevada* and *West Virginia*, *YT-146* stood by *Arizona* fighting fires until December 9.

The *Bagaduce*-class fleet tugs *Keosanqua* (AT-38) and *Sunnadin* (AT-28) were busy during the attack. *Keosanqua* was assisting *Antares* outside the harbor entrance with its tow and was strafed by Japanese planes. The tug suffered bullet holes, but no casualties. Tug *YT-153* was waiting for *Antares* and *Keosanqua* inside the harbor with a pilot. When the attack started and Antares remained outside of the harbor, *YT-153* turned and went to *Nevada*'s aid, fighting fires and helping to beach the battleship.

Sunnadin was underway at 9 a.m. to assist the battleship *Nevada* in moving away from her berth. Thirty minutes later, *Sunnadin* stood by *Pennsylvania* in case the battleship was to be moved from dry dock. When it became apparent that the dock would be flooded but the battleship would remain where it was, *Sunnadin* again went to *Nevada*'s aid as she was going aground at Hospital Point.

In a December 20, 1941, report, the Captain of the Yard summed up the performance of the men who rushed in to render aid to stricken vessels and rescue survivors in the water by saying: "There are undoubtedly many cases deserving of special commendation who have not been specifically mentioned. The personnel as a whole performed heroic service to the utmost of their ability and there are no reported cases of delinquency. There was no hesitation on the part of any tug master to either place his tug where told, or where he felt it would do the greatest good."

The following day *YG-21* aides the firefighting efforts on *Arizona*. NH 83062

Two days after the attack, the *Lapwing*-class minesweeper *Tern* (AM-31) is seen alongside *Arizona* after having fought fires on the battleship. When the attack began, *Tern* was undergoing refit and repairs, getting electricity from the dock. The minesweeper was made ready to sail and soon rescued forty-seven survivors from the water before she went to fight shipboard fires. NH 83063

APPENDIX A

U.S. SHIPS AT PEARL HARBOR AND VICINITY, DECEMBER 7, 1941, 8 A.M.

Ships listed by hull number. Asterisk denotes ships sunk during the air raid. *Arizona, Oklahoma,* and *Utah* were not returned to service. Source: NHHC

BATTLESHIP

Pennsylvania (BB-38—in drydock)
Arizona (BB-39)*
Nevada (BB-36)
Oklahoma (BB-37)*
Tennessee (BB-43)
California (BB-44)*
Maryland (BB-46)
West Virginia (BB-48)*

HEAVY CRUISER

New Orleans (CA-32)
San Francisco (CA-38)

LIGHT CRUISER

Raleigh (CL-7)
Detroit (CL-8)
Phoenix (CL-46)
Honolulu (CL-48)
St. Louis (CL-49)
Helena (CL-50)

DESTROYER

Allen (DD-66)
Schley (DD-103)
Chew (DD-106)
Ward (DD-139, patrolling Channel entrance to Pearl Harbor)
Dewey (DD-349)
Farragut (DD-348)
Hull (DD-350)
MacDonough (DD-351)
Worden (DD-352)
Dale (DD-353)

Monaghan (DD-354)
Aylwin (DD-355)
Selfridge (DD-357)
Phelps (DD-360)
Cummings (DD-365)
Reid (DD-369)
Case (DD-370)
Conyngham (DD-371)
Cassin (DD-372—in drydock)
Shaw (DD-373—in floating dry dock)
Tucker (DD-374)
Downes (DD-375—in dry dock)
Bagley (DD-386)
Blue (DD-387)
Helm (DD-388)
Mugford (DD-389)
Ralph Talbot (DD-390)
Henley (DD-391)
Patterson (DD-392)
Jarvis (DD-393)

SUBMARINE

Narwhal (SS-167)
Dolphin (SS-169)
Cachalot (SS-170)
Tautog (SS-199)

MINELAYER

Oglala (CM-4)*

MINESWEEPER

Turkey (AM-13)
Bobolink (AM-20)
Rail (AM-26)
Tern (AM-31)
Grebe (AM-43)
Vireo (AM-52)

COASTAL MINESWEEPER
Cockatoo (AMc-8)
Crossbill (AMc-9)
Condor (AMc-14)
Reedbird (AMc-30)

DESTROYER MINELAYER
Gamble (DM-15)
Ramsay (DM-16)
Montgomery (DM-17)
Breese (DM-18)
Tracy (DM-19)
Preble (DM-20)
Sicard (DM-21)
Pruitt (DM-22)

DESTROYER MINESWEEPER
Zane (DMS-14)
Wasmuth (DMS-15)
Trever (DMS-16)
Perry (DMS-17)

PATROL GUNBOAT
Sacramento (PG-19)

PATROL TORPEDO
PT-20, PT-21, PT-22, PT-23, PT-24, PT-25, PT-26, PT-27, PT-28, PT-29, PT-30, PT-42

DESTROYER TENDER
Dobbin (AD-3)
Whitney (AD-4)

SEAPLANE TENDER
Curtiss (AV-4)
Tangier (AV-8)

SMALL SEAPLANE TENDER
Avocet (AVP-4)
Swan (AVP-7, on marine railway dock)

SEAPLANE TENDER, DESTROYER
Hulbert (AVD-6)
Thornton (AVD-11)

AMMUNITION SHIP
Pyro (AE-1)

OILER
Ramapo (AO-12)
Neosho (AO-23)

REPAIR SHIP
Medusa (AR-1)
Vestal (AR-4)
Rigel (AR-11)

SUBMARINE TENDER
Pelias (AS-14)

SUBMARINE RESCUE SHIP
Widgeon (ASR-1)

HOSPITAL SHIP
Solace (AH-5)

STORES ISSUE SHIP
Castor (AKS-1)
Antares (AKS-3, at Pearl Harbor entrance)

OCEAN TUG
Ontario (AT-13)
Sunnadin (AT-28)
Keosanqua (AT-38, at Pearl Harbor entrance)
Navajo (AT-64, 12 miles outside Pearl Harbor entrance)

MISCELLANEOUS AUXILIARY
Utah (AG-16)*
Argonne (AG-31)
Sumner (AG-32)

APPENDIX B

PEARL HARBOR ATTACK MEDAL OF HONOR RECIPIENTS

Of the thousands of servicemen and women at bases on Oahu on the morning of December 7, 1941, and their countless acts of bravery and heroism, fourteen men were recognized for their actions with America's highest military award, the Medal of Honor. Nine were recognized posthumously. The text of their Medal of Honor citations is presented here.

Bennion, Mervyn S. (posthumous), Captain, U.S. Navy
USS *West Virginia*, Pearl Harbor, December 7, 1941

For conspicuous devotion to duty, extraordinary courage, and complete disregard of his own life, above and beyond the call of duty, during the attack on the Fleet in Pearl Harbor, by Japanese forces on 7 December 1941. As Commanding Officer of the U.S.S. *West Virginia*, after being mortally wounded, Capt. Bennion evidenced apparent concern only in fighting and saving his ship, and strongly protested against being carried from the bridge.

Finn, John W., Lieutenant, U.S. Navy
Naval Air Station, Kaneohe Bay, December 7, 1941

For extraordinary heroism distinguished service, and devotion above and beyond the call of duty. During the first attack by Japanese airplanes on the Naval Air Station, Kaneohe Bay, on 7 December 1941, Lt. Finn promptly secured and manned a 0.50-cal. machine gun mounted on an instruction stand in a completely exposed section of the parking ramp, which was under heavy enemy machinegun strafing fire. Although painfully wounded many times, he continued to man this gun and to return the enemy's fire vigorously and with telling effect throughout the enemy strafing and bombing attacks and with complete disregard for his own personal safety. It was only by specific orders that he was persuaded to leave his post to seek medical attention. Following first aid treatment, although obviously suffering much pain and moving with great difficulty, he returned to the squadron area and actively supervised the rearming of returning planes. His extraordinary heroism and conduct in this action were in keeping with the highest traditions of the U.S. Naval Service.

Flaherty, Francis C. (posthumous), Ensign, U.S. Naval Reserve
USS *Oklahoma*, Pearl Harbor, December 7, 1941

For conspicuous devotion to duty and extraordinary courage and complete disregard of his own life, above and beyond the call of duty, during the attack on the Fleet in Pearl Harbor, by Japanese forces on 7 December 1941. When it was seen that the U.S.S. *Oklahoma* was going to capsize and the order was given to abandon ship, Ens. Flaherty remained in a turret, holding a flashlight so the remainder of the turret crew could see to escape, thereby sacrificing his own life.

Fuqua, Samuel G., Captain (then lieutenant commander), U.S. Navy
USS *Arizona*, Pearl Harbor, December 7, 1941

For distinguished conduct in action, outstanding heroism, and utter disregard of his own safety above and beyond the call of duty during the attack on the Fleet in Pearl Harbor, by Japanese forces on 7 December 1941. Upon the commencement of the attack, Lt. Comdr. Fuqua rushed to the quarterdeck of the U.S.S. *Arizona* to which he was attached where he was stunned and knocked down by the explosion of a large bomb, which hit the quarter deck, penetrated several decks, and started a severe fire.

Upon regaining consciousness, he began to direct the fighting of the fire and the rescue of wounded and injured personnel. Almost immediately there was a tremendous explosion forward, which made the ship appear to rise out of the water, shudder, and settle down by the bow rapidly. The whole forward part of the ship was enveloped in flames which were spreading rapidly, and wounded and burned men were pouring out of the ship to the quarterdeck. Despite these conditions, his harrowing experience, and severe enemy bombing and strafing, at the time, Lt. Comdr. Fuqua continued to direct the fighting of fires in order to check them while the wounded and burned could be taken from the ship and supervised the rescue of these men in such an amazingly calm and cool manner and with such excellent judgment that it inspired everyone who saw him and undoubtedly resulted in the saving of many lives.

After realizing the ship could not be saved and that he was the senior surviving officer aboard, he directed it to be abandoned, but continued to remain on the quarterdeck and directed abandoning ship and rescue of personnel until satisfied that all personnel that could be had been saved, after which he left his ship with the boatload. The conduct of Lt. Comdr. Fuqua was not only in keeping with the highest traditions of the naval service but characterizes him as an outstanding leader of men.

Hill, Edwin J. (posthumous), Chief Boatswain, U.S. Navy
USS *Nevada*, Pearl Harbor, T.H., December 7, 1941

For distinguished conduct in the line of his profession, extraordinary courage, and disregard of his own safety during the attack on the Fleet in Pearl Harbor, by Japanese forces on 7 December 1941. During the height of the strafing and bombing, Chief Boatswain Hill led his men of the linehandling details of the U.S.S. *Nevada* to the quays, cast off the lines and swam back to his ship. Later, while on the forecastle, attempting to let go the anchors, he was blown overboard and killed by the explosion of several bombs.

Jones, Herbert C. (posthumous), Ensign, U.S. Naval Reserve
USS *California*, Pearl Harbor, December 7, 1941

For conspicuous devotion to duty, extraordinary courage, and complete disregard of his own life, above and beyond the call of duty, during the attack on the Fleet in Pearl Harbor, by Japanese forces on 7 December 1941. Ens. Jones organized and led a party, which was supplying ammunition to the antiaircraft battery of the U.S.S. *California* after the mechanical hoists were put out of action when he was fatally wounded by a bomb explosion. When 2 men attempted to take him from the area which was on fire, he refused to let them do so, saying in words to the effect, "Leave me alone! I am done for. Get out of here before the magazines go off."

Pharris, Jackson C., Lieutenant (then gunner), U.S. Navy
USS *California*, Pearl Harbor, December 7, 1941

For conspicuous gallantry and intrepidity at the risk of his life above and beyond the call of duty while attached to the U.S.S. *California* during the surprise enemy Japanese aerial attack on Pearl Harbor, Territory of Hawaii, 7 December 1941.

In charge of the ordnance repair party on the third deck when the first Japanese torpedo struck almost directly under his station, Lt. (then Gunner) Pharris was stunned and severely injured by the concussion which hurled him to the overhead and back to the deck. Quickly recovering, he acted on his own initiative to set up a hand-supply ammunition train for the antiaircraft guns. With water and oil rushing in where the port bulkhead had been torn up from the deck, with many of the remaining crewmembers overcome by oil fumes, and the ship without power and listing heavily to port as a result of a second torpedo hit, Lt. Pharris ordered the shipfitters to counterflood. Twice rendered unconscious by the nauseous fumes and handicapped by his painful injuries, he persisted in his desperate efforts to speed up the supply of ammunition and at the same time repeatedly risked his life to enter flooding compartments and drag to safety unconscious shipmates who were gradually being submerged in oil.

By his inspiring leadership, his valiant efforts and his extreme loyalty to his ship and her crew, he saved many of his shipmates from death and was largely responsible for keeping the *California* in action during the attack. His heroic conduct throughout this first eventful engagement of World War 11 reflects the highest credit upon Lt. Pharris and enhances the finest traditions of the U.S. Naval Service.

Reeves, Thomas J. (posthumous), Radio Electrician (Warrant Officer), U.S. Navy
USS *California*, Pearl Harbor, December 7, 1941

For distinguished conduct in the line of his profession, extraordinary courage and disregard of his own safety during the attack on the Fleet in Pearl Harbor, by Japanese forces on 7 December 1941. After the mechanized ammunition hoists were put out of action in the U.S.S. *California*, Reeves, on his own initiative, in a burning passageway, assisted in the maintenance of an ammunition supply by hand to the antiaircraft guns until he was overcome by smoke and fire, which resulted in his death.

Ross, Donald K., Machinist, U.S. Navy
USS *Nevada*, Pearl Harbor, December 7, 1941

For distinguished conduct in the line of his profession, extraordinary courage and disregard of his own life during the attack on the Fleet in Pearl Harbor, Territory of Hawaii, by Japanese forces on 7 December 1941. When his station in the forward dynamo room of the U.S.S. *Nevada* became almost untenable due to smoke, steam, and heat, Warrant Machinist Ross forced his men to leave that station and performed all the duties himself until blinded and unconscious. Upon being rescued and resuscitated, he returned and secured the forward dynamo room and proceeded to the after dynamo room where he was later again rendered unconscious by exhaustion. Again recovering consciousness he returned to his station where he remained until directed to abandon it.

Scott, Robert R. (posthumous), Machinist's Mate First Class, U.S. Navy
USS *California*, Pearl Harbor, December 7, 1941

For conspicuous devotion to duty, extraordinary courage and complete disregard of his own life, above and beyond the call of duty, during the attack on the Fleet in Pearl Harbor by Japanese forces on 7 December 1941. The compartment, in the U.S.S. *California*, in which the air compressor, to which Scott was assigned as his battle station, was flooded as the result of a torpedo hit. The remainder of the personnel evacuated that compartment but Scott refused to leave, saying words to the effect, "This is my station and I will stay and give them air as long as the guns are going."

Tomich, Peter (posthumous), Chief Watertender, U.S. Navy
USS *Utah*, Pearl Harbor, December 7, 1941

For distinguished conduct in the line of his profession, and extraordinary courage and disregard of his own safety, during the attack on the Fleet in Pearl Harbor by the Japanese forces on 7 December 1941. Although realizing that the ship was capsizing, as a result of enemy bombing and torpedoing, Tomich remained at his post in the engineering plant of the U.S.S. *Utah*, until he saw that all boilers were secured and all fireroom personnel had left their stations, and by so doing lost his own life .

Van Valkenburgh, Franklin (posthumous), Captain, U.S. Navy
USS *Arizona*, Pearl Harbor, December 7, 1941

For conspicuous devotion to duty, extraordinary courage and complete disregard of his own life, during the attack on the Fleet in Pearl Harbor T.H., by Japanese forces on 7 December 1941. As commanding officer of the U.S.S. *Arizona*, Capt. Van Valkenburgh gallantly fought his ship until the U.S.S. *Arizona* blew up from magazine explosions and a direct bomb hit on the bridge which resulted in the loss of his life.

Ward, James R. (posthumous), Seaman First Class, U.S. Navy
USS *Oklahoma*, Pearl Harbor, December 7, 1941

For conspicuous devotion to duty, extraordinary courage and complete disregard of his life, above and beyond the call of duty, during the attack on the Fleet in Pearl Harbor by Japanese forces on 7 December 1941. When it was seen that the U.S.S. *Oklahoma* was going to capsize and the order was given to abandon ship, Ward remained in a turret holding a flashlight so the remainder of the turret crew could see to escape, thereby sacrificing his own life.

Young, Cassin, Commander, U.S. Navy
USS *Vestal*, Pearl Harbor, December 7, 1941

For distinguished conduct in action, outstanding heroism and utter disregard of his own safety, above and beyond the call of duty, as commanding officer of the U.S.S. *Vestal*, during the attack on the Fleet in Pearl Harbor, Territory of Hawaii, by enemy Japanese forces on 7 December 1941. Comdr. Young proceeded to the bridge and later took personal command of the 3-inch antiaircraft gun. When blown overboard by the blast of the forward magazine explosion of the U.S.S. *Arizona*, to which the U.S.S. *Vestal* was moored, he swam back to his ship. The entire forward part of the U.S.S. *Arizona* was a blazing inferno with oil afire on the water between the two ships; as a result of several bomb hits, the U.S.S. *Vestal* was afire in several places, was settling and taking on a list. Despite severe enemy bombing and strafing at the time, and his shocking experience of having been blown overboard, Comdr. Young, with extreme coolness and calmness, moved his ship to an anchorage distant from the U.S.S. *Arizona*, and subsequently beached the U.S.S. *Vestal* upon determining that such action was required to save his ship.

APPENDIX C

DIRECTORY OF SELECTED SHIPS IN PORT ON DECEMBER 7, 1941

U.S. NAVY

NAVAL HISTORY AND HERITAGE COMMAND NH61483

NHHC 19-N-28341

BATTLESHIPS

Arizona (BB-39)
    Class: *Pennsylvania*
    Commissioned: October 17, 1916
    Crew: 1,081
    Length: 608 feet
    Beam: 97 feet, 1 inch
    Draft: 28 feet, 10 inches
    Displacement: 31,400 tons
    Speed: 21 knots
    Armament: 12 x 14-inch guns; 22 x 5-inch guns;
4 x 3-inch guns; 2 x 21-inch torpedo tubes

California (BB-44)
    Class: *Tennessee*
    Commissioned: August 10, 1921
    Crew: 1,083
    Length: 624 feet, 6 inches
    Beam: 97 feet, 4 inches
    Draft: 30 feet, 3 inches
    Displacement: 32,300 tons
    Speed: 21 knots
    Armament: 12 x 14-inch guns, 14 x 5-inch guns,
4 x 3-inch guns, 2 x 21-inch torpedo tubes

Maryland (BB-46)
    Class: *Colorado*
    Commissioned: July 21, 1921
    Crew: 1,080
    Length: 624 feet
    Beam: 97 feet, 6 inches
    Draft: 30 feet, 6 inches
    Displacement: 32,600 tons
    Speed: 21.17 knots
    Armament: 8 x 16-inch guns, 12 x 5-inch guns,
4 x 3-inch guns, 4 x 6-pounder guns (2.2 inch),
2 x 21-inch torpedo tubes

NHHC NH97395

Nevada (BB-36)
   Class: *Nevada*
   Commissioned: March 11, 1916
   Crew: 864
   Length: 583 feet
   Beam: 85 feet, 3 inches
   Draft: 28 feet, 6 inches
   Displacement: 27,500 tons
   Speed: 20.5 knots
   Armament: 10 x 14-inch guns, 21 x 5-inch guns,
4 x 21-inch torpedo tubes

NHHC NH77076

Oklahoma (BB-37)
   Class: *Nevada*
   Commissioned: May 2, 1916
   Crew: 864
   Length: 583 feet
   Beam: 85 feet, 3 inches
   Draft: 28 feet, 6 inches
   Displacement: 27,500 tons
   Speed: 20.5 knots
   Armament: 10 x 14-inch guns, 21 x 5-inch guns,
4 x 21-inch torpedo tubes

NHHC NH67583

Pennsylvania (BB-38)
   Class: *Pennsylvania*
   Commissioned: June 12, 1916
   Crew: 915
   Length: 608 feet
   Beam: 97 feet, 1 inch
   Draft: 28 feet, 10 inches
   Displacement: 31,400 tons
   Speed: 21 knots
   Armament: 12 x 14-inch guns, 14 x 5-inch guns,
4 x 3-inch guns, 4 x 3-pounder guns (1.9 inch or
47mm), 2 x 21-inch torpedo tubes

NATIONAL ARCHIVES 80G-456336

Tennessee (BB-43)
   Class: *Tennessee*
   Commissioned: June 3, 1920
   Crew: 1,401
   Length: 624 feet
   Beam: 97 feet, 3 inches
   Draft: 31 feet
   Displacement: 33,190 tons
   Speed: 21 knots
   Armament: 12 x 14-inch guns, 14 x 5-inch guns,
4 x 3-inch guns, 2 x 21-inch torpedo tubes

NATIONAL ARCHIVES 80G-1027204

West Virginia (BB-48)
    Class: *Colorado*
    Commissioned: December 1, 1923
    Crew: 1,407
    Length: 624 feet
    Beam: 97 feet, 3 inches
    Draft: 30 feet, 6 inches
    Displacement: 33,590 tons
    Speed: 21 knots
    Armament: 8 x 16-inch guns, 12 x 5-inch guns,
4 x 3-inch guns, 2 x 21-inch torpedo tubes

CRUISERS

WILLIAM T. LARKINS COLLECTION

Detroit (CL-8)
    Class: *Omaha*
    Commissioned: July 31, 1923
    Crew: 458
    Length: 555 feet, 6 inches
    Beam: 55 feet, 4 inches
    Draft: 13 feet, 6 inches
    Displacement: 7,050 tons
    Speed: 34 knots
    Armament: 12 x 6-inch guns, 4 x 3-inch guns,
10 x 21-inch torpedo tubes

NHHC NH64621

Raleigh (CL-7)
    Class: *Omaha*
    Commissioned: July 31, 1923
    Crew: 458
    Length: 555 feet, 6 inches
    Beam: 55 feet, 4 inches
    Draft: 13 feet, 6 inches
    Displacement: 7,050 tons
    Speed: 34 knots
    Armament: 12 x 6-inch guns, 4 x 3-inch guns,
10 x 21-inch torpedo tubes

NHHC NH60326

Phoenix (CL-46)
    Class: *Brooklyn*
    Commissioned: October 3, 1938
    Crew: 868
    Length: 608 feet, 4 inches
    Beam: 61 feet, 9 inches
    Draft: 19 feet, 5 inches
    Displacement: 10,000 tons
    Speed: 33.6 knots
    Armament: 15 x 6-inch guns, 8 x 5-inch
anti-aircraft guns, 8 x 0.50-cal. machine guns.

NATIONAL ARCHIVES 80G-451205

Honolulu (CL-48)
    Class: *Brooklyn*
    Commissioned: June 15, 1938
    Crew: 868
    Length: 608 feet, 4 inches
    Beam: 61 feet, 9 inches
    Draft: 19 feet, 5 inches
    Displacement: 10,000 tons
    Speed: 33.6 knots
    Armament: 15 x 6-inch guns (150mm), 8 x 5-inch
anti-aircraft guns, 8 x 0.50-cal. machine guns.

NHHC NH95815

Helena (CL-50)
    Class: *St. Louis*
    Commissioned: September 18, 1939
    Crew: 888
    Length: 608 feet, 4 inches
    Beam: 61 feet, 8 inches
    Draft: 19 feet, 10 inches
    Displacement: 10,000 tons
    Speed: 32.5 knots
    Armament: 15 x 6-inch guns, 8 x 5-inch guns,
8 x 0.50-cal. machine guns

NHHC NH80393

DESTROYERS

Chew (DD-106)
    Class: *Wickes*
    Commissioned: December 12, 1918
    Crew: 113
    Length: 314 feet, 5 inches
    Beam: 31 feet, 9 inches
    Draft: 8 feet, 6 inches
    Displacement: 1,060 tons
    Speed: 35 knots
    Armament: 4 x 4-inch guns, 12 x 21-inch torpedo
tubes

Ward (DD-139)
    Class: *Wickes*
    Commissioned: July 24, 1918
    Crew: 231
    Length: 314 feet, 4 inches
    Beam: 30 feet, 11 inches
    Draft: 9 feet, 10 inches
    Displacement: 1,247 long tons
    Speed: 35 knots
    Armament: 4 x 4-inch guns, 2 x 3-inch guns,
12 x 21-inch torpedo tubes

NHHC NH97328

Cassin (DD-372)

Class: *Mahan* Class—18 ships, including *Downes* (DD-375), *Shaw* (DD-372)

Commissioned: August 21, 1936

Crew: 158

Length: 341 feet, 4 inches

Beam: 35 feet

Draft: 9 feet, 10 inches

Displacement: 1,500 long tons

Speed: 36 knots

Armament: 5 x 5-inch guns, 12 x 21-inch torpedo tubes

NATIONAL ARCHIVES 80G-266840

Helm (DD-388)

Class: *Gridley*

Commissioned: October 16, 1937

Crew: 200

Length: 341 feet, 8 inches

Beam: 34 feet, 8 inches

Draft: 9 feet, 10 inches

Displacement: 1,500 tons

Speed: 36.5 knots

Armament: 4 x 5-inch guns, 4 x 0.50-cal machine guns, 12 x 21-inch torpedo tubes.

NHHC NH55535

AUXILIARIES

Curtiss (AV-4)

Class: *Curtiss*

Commissioned: November 15, 1940

Crew: 1,195

Length: 527 feet, 4 inches

Beam: 69 feet, 3 inches

Draft: 21 feet, 11 inches

Speed: 20 knots

Displacement: 8,671 tons

Armament: one 5-inch/38 gun, three quad 40mm AA guns, two twin 40mm AA gun mounts

NHHC NH60281

Oglala (CM-4)

Converted steamer built in 1907

Acquired by the U.S. Navy on November 9, 1917

Crew: 200

Length: 386 feet

Beam: 52 feet, 2 inches

Draft: 14 feet, 7 inches

Speed: 14 knots

Displacement: 3,806 tons

Armament: 300 mines, 1 x 5-inch gun, 4 x 3-inch guns, 4 x 40mm, 8 x 20mm

U.S. NAVY

Utah (AG-16)

    Class: *Florida*

    Commissioned: August 31, 1911

    Crew: 525

    Length: 521 feet, 6 inches

    Beam: 88 feet, 3 inches

    Draft: 28 feet, 4 inches

    Speed: 20.75 knots

    Displacement: 21,825 tons

NHHC NH50272

Vestal (AR-4)

    Class: *Vestal*

    Commissioned: October 4, 1909

    Crew: 90

    Length: 465 feet, 9 inches

    Beam: 60 feet, 1 inch

    Draft: 26 feet

    Speed: 16 knots

    Displacement: 12,585 tons

SUBMARINES

Narwahl (SS-167)

    Class: *Narwahl*

    Commissioned: May 15, 1930

    Crew: 88

    Length: 371 feet

    Beam: 33 feet, 3 inches

    Draft: 15 feet, 9 inches

    Displacement: 2,730 tons (surfaced), 3,960 tons (submerged)

    Speed: 17 knots (surfaced), 8 knots (submerged)

    Armament: 2 x 6-inch guns, 2 x 0.30-cal. machine guns, 10 x 21-inch torpedo tubes

NATIONAL ARCHIVES 80G-418413

APPENDIX D

U.S. NAVY AIRCRAFT DESTROYED, DECEMBER 7, 1941

The U.S. Navy lost 92 aircraft during the air raid, plus an additional 8 aircraft lost later in the day. The list that follows contains the 100 aircraft lost on December 7, 1941.

Type	Buno	Unit	Location
F2A-3	1544	VF-2	USS *Lexington* (CV-2)
F2A-3	1507	VMF-221	Ewa Field
F4F-3	3906	VF-6	USS *Enterprise* (CV-6)
	3909	VF-6	USS *Enterprise* (CV-6)
	3935	VF-6	USS *Enterprise* (CV-6)
	3938	VF-6	USS *Enterprise* (CV-6)
	3977	VMF-211	Ewa Field
	3992	VMF-211	Ewa Field
	4018	VMF-211	Ewa Field
	4023	VMF-211	Ewa Field
	4025	VMF-211	Ewa Field
	4029	VMF-211	Ewa Field
	4034	VMF-211	Ewa Field
	4040	VMF-211	Ewa Field
J2F-4	1644	VMJ-252	Ewa Field
J2F-4	1656	VMJ-252	Ewa Field
JO-2	1051	VMJ-252	Ewa Field
JRS-1	1061	VMJ-252	Ewa Field
OS2U-2	2199	Ship's Unit	USS *Curtiss* (AV-4)
OS2U-3	5285	VO-4	USS *Maryland* (BB-46)
	5288	VO-1	USS *Oklahoma* (BB-37)
	5289	VO-1	USS *Oklahoma* (BB-37)
	5290	VO-1	USS *Oklahoma* (BB-37)
	5294	VO-2	USS *Nevada* (BB-36)
	5305	VO-2	USS *Tennessee* (BB-43)
	5326	VO-4	USS *West Virginia* (BB-48)
	5327	VO-4	USS *West Virginia* (BB-48)

Type	Buno	Unit	Location
	5353	VO-2	USS *California* (BB-44)
PBY-3	852	VP-22	PatWing 2 - NAS Pearl Harbor
	853	VP-22	PatWing 2 - NAS Pearl Harbor
	873	VP-22	PatWing 2 - NAS Pearl Harbor
	874	VP-22	PatWing 2 - NAS Pearl Harbor
	875	VP-22	PatWing 2 - NAS Pearl Harbor
	882	VP-22	PatWing 2 - NAS Pearl Harbor
	898	VP-22	PatWing 2 - NAS Pearl Harbor
	899	VP-22	PatWing 2 - NAS Pearl Harbor
	900	VP-22	PatWing 2 - NAS Pearl Harbor
PBY-4	1226	VP-22	PatWing 2 - NAS Pearl Harbor
PBY-5	2291	VP-22	PatWing 2 - NAS Pearl Harbor
	2293	VP-22	PatWing 2 - NAS Pearl Harbor
	2301	VP-22	PatWing 2 - NAS Pearl Harbor
	2302	VP-22	PatWing 2 - NAS Pearl Harbor
	2303	VP-22	PatWing 2 - NAS Pearl Harbor
	2308	VP-22	PatWing 2 - NAS Pearl Harbor
	2357	VP-14	PatWing 1 - NAS Kaneohe Bay
	2359	VP-14	PatWing 1 - NAS Kaneohe Bay
	2361	VP-14	PatWing 1 - NAS Kaneohe Bay
	2362	VP-14	PatWing 1 - NAS Kaneohe Bay
	2364	VP-14	PatWing 1 - NAS Kaneohe Bay
	2365	VP-14	PatWing 1 - NAS Kaneohe Bay
	2369	VP-14	PatWing 1 - NAS Kaneohe Bay
	2420	VP-11	PatWing 1 - NAS Kaneohe Bay
	2421	VP-11	PatWing 1 - NAS Kaneohe Bay
	2422	VP-11	PatWing 1 - NAS Kaneohe Bay
	2423	VP-11	PatWing 1 - NAS Kaneohe Bay
	2425	VP-12	PatWing 1 - NAS Kaneohe Bay
	2429	VP-11	PatWing 1 - NAS Kaneohe Bay
	2430	VP-11	PatWing 1 - NAS Kaneohe Bay
	2431	VP-11	PatWing 1 - NAS Kaneohe Bay
	2434	VP-11	PatWing 1 - NAS Kaneohe Bay
	2435	VP-12	PatWing 1 - NAS Kaneohe Bay

Type	Buno	Unit	Location
	2436	VP-12	PatWing 1 - NAS Kaneohe Bay
	2437	VP-12	PatWing 1 - NAS Kaneohe Bay
	2439	VP-12	PatWing 1 - NAS Kaneohe Bay
	2440	VP-12	PatWing 1 - NAS Kaneohe Bay
	2441	VP-12	PatWing 1 - NAS Kaneohe Bay
	2444	VP-12	PatWing 1 - NAS Kaneohe Bay
	2445	VP-23	PatWing 2 - NAS Pearl Harbor
	2448	VP-23	PatWing 2 - NAS Pearl Harbor
	2451	VP-23	PatWing 2 - NAS Pearl Harbor
R3D-2	1904	VMJ-252	Ewa Field
SBD-1	1626	VMSB-232	Ewa Field
	1630	VMSB-232	Ewa Field
	1736	VMSB-232	Ewa Field
	1737	VMSB-232	Ewa Field
	1744	VMSB-232	Ewa Field
	1745	VMSB-232	Ewa Field
	1746	VMSB-232	Ewa Field
	1752	VMSB-232	Ewa Field
	1753	VMSB-232	Ewa Field
SBD-2	2110	VMSB-232	Ewa Field
	2112	VB-2	USS *Lexington* (CV-2)
	2146	VS-2	USS *Lexington* (CV-2)
	2158	VB-6	USS *Enterprise* (CV-6)
	2159	VB-6	USS *Enterprise* (CV-6)
	2160	VB-6	USS *Enterprise* (CV-6)
	2161	VB-6	USS *Enterprise* (CV-6)
	2181	VB-6	USS *Enterprise* (CV-6)

Type	Buno	Unit	Location
SBD-3	4570	VS-6	USS *Enterprise* (CV-6)
	4572	VS-6	USS *Enterprise* (CV-6)
	4639	VS-2	USS *Lexington* (CV-2)
SB2U-3	2047	VMSB-231	Ewa Field
	2050	VMSB-231	Ewa Field
	2051	VMSB-231	Ewa Field
	2060	VMSB-231	Ewa Field
	2063	VMSB-231	Ewa Field
	2068	VMSB-231	Ewa Field
	2069	VMSB-231	Ewa Field
	2070	VMJ-252	Ewa Field
SNJ-3	6794	VMJ-252	Ewa Field

Source: Individual Aircraft Record Cards, Aircraft Accident Reports, and information supplied by Craig Fuller of Aviation Archaeological Investigation and Research (www. aviationarchaeology.com).

APPENDIX E

U.S. ARMY AIR FORCES AIRCRAFT DESTROYED, DECEMBER 7, 1941

Type	s/n	Unit Assigned	Location
A-20A	40-137	58th Bomb Squadron (Light)	Hickam Field
	40-151	58th Bomb Squadron (Light)	Hickam Field
B-17C	40-2049	38th Reconnaissance Squadron	Bellows Field
	40-2074	38th Reconnaissance Squadron	Hickam Field
B-17D	40-3060	11th Bomb Group	Hickam Field
	40-3071	5th Bomb Group	Hickam Field
	40-3077	11th Bomb Group	Hickam Field
	40-3080	5th Bomb Group	Hickam Field
	40-3081	11th Bomb Group	Hickam Field
	40-3083	11th Bomb Group	Hickam Field
B-18	36-270	11th Bomb Group	Hickam Field
	36-272	Hawaiian Air Depot	Hickam Field
	36-331	Hawaiian Air Depot	Hickam Field
	36-335	Hawaiian Air Depot	Hickam Field
	36-442	Hickam Field	Hickam Field
	37-3	5th Bomb Group	Hickam Field
	37-4	5th Bomb Group	Hickam Field
	37-7	11th Bomb Group	Hickam Field
	37-11	5th Bomb Group	Hickam Field
	37-12	5th Bomb Group	Hickam Field
	37-19	5th Bomb Group	Hickam Field
B-24A	40-2371	44th Bomb Group	Hickam Field
P-26A	33-37	78th Pursuit Sqn., 18th Pursuit Group	Wheeler Field
	33-39	78th Pursuit Sqn., 18th Pursuit Group	Wheeler Field
	33-68	44th Pursuit Sqn., 18th Pursuit Group	Wheeler Field
	33-80	78th Pursuit Sqn., 18th Pursuit Group	Wheeler Field
	33-86	6th Pursuit Sqn., 18th Pursuit Group	Wheeler Field
P-26B	33-180	6th Pursuit Sqn., 18th Pursuit Group	Wheeler Field
P-36A	38-63	45th Pursuit Sqn. 15th Pursuit Group	Wheeler Field
	38-118	46th Pursuit Sqn. 15th Pursuit Group	Wheeler Field

Type	s/n	Unit Assigned	Location
	38-124	46th Pursuit Sqn. 15th Pursuit Group	Wheeler Field
	38-176	45th Pursuit Sqn. 15th Pursuit Group	Wheeler Field
P-40B	41-5208	Hawaiian Air Depot	Hickam Field
	41-5209	Hawaiian Air Depot	Hickam Field
	41-5212	6th Pursuit Sqn., 18th Pursuit Group	Wheeler Field
	41-5215	6th Pursuit Sqn., 18th Pursuit Group	Wheeler Field
	41-5217	6th Pursuit Sqn., 18th Pursuit Group	Wheeler Field
	41-5218	19th Pursuit Sqn., 18th Pursuit Group	Wheeler Field
	41-5219	6th Pursuit Sqn., 18th Pursuit Group	Wheeler Field
	41-5222	6th Pursuit Sqn., 18th Pursuit Group	Wheeler Field
	41-5223	6th Pursuit Sqn., 18th Pursuit Group	Wheeler Field
	41-5225	6th Pursuit Sqn., 18th Pursuit Group	Wheeler Field
	41-5226	73rd Pursuit Sqn., 18th Pursuit Group	Wheeler Field
	41-5227	19th Pursuit Sqn., 18th Pursuit Group	Wheeler Field
	41-5231	73rd Pursuit Sqn., 18th Pursuit Group	Wheeler Field
	41-5232	6th Pursuit Sqn., 18th Pursuit Group	Wheeler Field
	41-5233	73rd Pursuit Sqn., 18th Pursuit Group	Wheeler Field
	41-5235	73rd Pursuit Sqn., 18th Pursuit Group	Wheeler Field
	41-5237	73rd Pursuit Sqn., 18th Pursuit Group	Wheeler Field
	41-5242	73rd Pursuit Sqn., 18th Pursuit Group	Wheeler Field
	41-5244	78th Pursuit Sqn., 18th Pursuit Group	Wheeler Field
	41-5246	78th Pursuit Sqn., 18th Pursuit Group	Wheeler Field
	41-5247	19th Pursuit Sqn., 18th Pursuit Group	Wheeler Field
	41-5250	78th Pursuit Sqn., 18th Pursuit Group	Wheeler Field
	41-5251	78th Pursuit Sqn., 18th Pursuit Group	Wheeler Field
	41-5252	78th Pursuit Sqn., 18th Pursuit Group	Wheeler Field
	41-5253	Hawaiian Air Depot	Wheeler Field
	41-5257	78th Pursuit Sqn., 18th Pursuit Group	Wheeler Field
	41-5291	6th Pursuit Sqn., 18th Pursuit Group	Wheeler Field
	41-5299	6th Pursuit Sqn., 18th Pursuit Group	Wheeler Field
	41-5300	wrecked in depot shops	Wheeler Field
	41-5304	19th Pursuit Sqn., 18th Pursuit Group	Wheeler Field
	41-13299	73rd Pursuit Sqn., 18th Pursuit Group	Wheeler Field

Type	s/n	Unit Assigned	Location
	41-13300	73rd Pursuit Sqn., 18th Pursuit Group	Wheeler Field
	41-13303	19th Pursuit Sqn., 18th Pursuit Group	Wheeler Field
	41-13310	19th Pursuit Sqn., 18th Pursuit Group	Wheeler Field
	41-13312	78th Pursuit Sqn., 18th Pursuit Group	Wheeler Field
	41-13317	47th Pursuit Sqn., 15th Pursuit Group	Wheeler Field
	41-13320	44th Pursuit Sqn, 18th Pursuit Group	Wheeler Field
	41-13324	47th Pursuit Sqn., 15th Pursuit Group	Wheeler Field
P-40C	41-13328	44th Pursuit Sqn, 18th Pursuit Group	Wheeler Field
	41-13330	19th Pursuit Sqn, 44th Pursuit Group	Wheeler Field
	41-13331	44th Pursuit Sqn, 18th Pursuit Group	Wheeler Field
	41-13337	44th Pursuit Sqn, 18th Pursuit Group	Bellows Field
OA-9	38-558	18th Air Base Group	Wheeler Field
	38-575	Headquarters Sqn., 18th Pursuit Group	Wheeler Field
O-49	40-218	Hawaiian Air Depot	Hickam Field

The following aircraft were damaged or destroyed prior to December 7, 1941, but were held as a source of spare parts. These aircraft were written off by the Hawaiian Air Depot on December 28, 1941, along with the aircraft destroyed in the Pearl Harbor attack:

Model	Serial	Pilot	Date of accident
P-40B	41-5211	2Lt Sidney F. Wharton	7/07/41
6th Pursuit Sqn., 18th Pursuit Grp., Bellows Field,				
P-40B	41-5214	2Lt Ingram O'Connor, Jr.	4/21/41
6th Pursuit Sqn., 18th Pursuit Group				
P-40B	41-5216	2Lt D. O'Connor	4/16/41
19th Pursuit Sqn., 18th Pursuit Group				
P-40B	41-5220	2Lt Jesse W. Haynes	9/16/41
6th Pursuit Sqn., 18th Pursuit Group				
P-40B	41-5228	Francis W. Potts	6/09/41
73rd Pursuit Sqn., 18th Pursuit Group				
P-40B	41-5229	1Lt Joseph A. Morris	9/23/41
73rd Pursuit Sqn., 18th Pursuit Group				

The following seven P-40Bs were rebuilt after the Japanese attack and returned to service:

41-5223
41-5231
41-5237
41-5250
41-5251
41-5253
41-5304

Source: Individual Aircraft Record Cards, Aircraft Accident Reports, and information supplied by David Aiken (director, Pearl Harbor History Associates, Inc., www.pearlharbor. com), Craig Fuller of Aviation Archaeological Investigation and Research (www.aviation archaeology.com), David Trojan.

APPENDIX F

PEARL HARBOR MEMORIALS AND MUSEUMS

The following is a list of important historical sites and museums related to the Pearl Harbor Air Raid. Some venues charge a small fee per person to visit.

USS *ARIZONA* MEMORIAL (VALOR IN THE PACIFIC NATIONAL MONUMENT)

The National Park Service operates the USS *Arizona* Memorial as part of the Valor in the Pacific National Monument. The Pearl Harbor site includes a visitors center and boat tours to the USS *Arizona* Memorial spanning the battleship's hull. If you are visiting, tickets are free, but you must either pick up a physical ticket or make an online reservation. More information is available at *www.nps.gov/valr/index.htm*.

BATTLESHIP *MISSOURI* MEMORIAL

It is an interesting dichotomy to stand on the USS *Arizona* Memorial above the grave of the ship that symbolizes the beginning of World War II for the United States and stare across the harbor waters to see the battleship *Missouri*, where the instrument of unconditional surrender was signed by the Japanese. On board the *Missouri*, guests can stand at the actual spot where the surrender was signed. On the web at *www.ussmissouri.org*.

USS *BOWFIN* SUBMARINE MUSEUM & PARK

The USS *Bowfin* Submarine Museum and Park is home to the submarine *Bowfin* and a memorial to the fifty-two U.S. submarines lost during World War II. *Bowfin* (SS-287) was nicknamed "The Pearl Harbor Avenger" as she was launched on December 7, 1942, at the Portsmouth Navy Yard in Maine one year after the Japanese attack. Visitors visit the museum to learn about submarine technology, the *Bowfin*'s nine war patrols, and more. Information about the submarine, museum, and memorial are at *www.bowfin.org*.

PACIFIC AVIATION MUSEUM—PEARL HARBOR

Pearl Harbor needed a museum dedicated to the aviation side of World War II and beyond. The museum is housed in Hangars 37 and 79, both of which survived the Japanese attack on Pearl Harbor. In addition to its historic location, the museum holds the remains of pilot Shigenori Nishikaichi's Zero fighter from *Hiryu* that was crash-landed on Niihau after the Pearl Harbor attack, an intact Zero fighter, and a Nakajima B5N Kate torpedo bomber—one of only two known survivors in the world. Other displays recall the Doolittle Raid, the Battle of Midway, aerial action in Korea, Vietnam, to the present day. Information on the museum is at *www.pacificaviationmuseum.org*.

PLANES OF FAME AIR MUSEUM

The largest collection of Japanese aircraft in the United States, outside the National Air and Space Museum, has been gathered by the Planes of Fame Air Museum in Chino, California. The Japanese aircraft collection includes an Aichi D3A2 Val, Mitsubishi A6M5 Zero, Mitsubishi J2M3 *Raiden*, Mitsubishi J8M1 *Shusui*, and Yokosuka D4Y3 *Suiseu*. Also on display and flying are examples of the American types present at Pearl Harbor: B-17, O-47, P-26, P-40, and SBD. The museum also hosts a warbird airshow every year in May. More information is available at *www.planesoffame.org*.

NATIONAL WORLD WAR II MEMORIAL

America's tribute to the more than 400,000 who died during World War II as well as to those who served in uniform and on the home front. This memorial is located on the National Mall in Washington, D.C. See *www.wwiimemorial.com* and *www.nps.gov/wwii/index.htm*.

NATIONAL MUSEUM OF THE UNITED STATES AIR FORCE

The history of the U.S. Air Force and its predecessor organizations is displayed at the museum in Dayton, Ohio. Of note is the Curtiss P-36A Hawk displayed in a diorama showing Lt. Philip Rasmussen boarding the aircraft to take the fight to the Japanese on the morning of December 7, 1941. More information at *www.nationalmuseum.af.mil.*

NATIONAL NAVAL AVIATION MUSEUM

Pensacola, Florida, is home to the National Naval Aviation Museum, which displays three of the American types present during the Pearl Harbor Air Raid, a Curtiss P-40B Tomahawk, SB2U Vindicator, SBD Dauntless. The museum also displays an A6M2 Zero of Pearl Harbor attack vintage and an N1K2 Shideni-Kai (Allied code name George) from later in the war. Details are online at *www.navalaviationmuseum.org.*

NATIONAL MUSEUM OF THE PACIFIC WAR

The Adm. Chester W. Nimitz Museum in Fredricksburg, Texas, has been expanded into the National Museum of the Pacific War. The museum holds many important documents and displays, including the Japanese midget submarine that beached on the reef off of Bellows Field the day after the Pearl Harbor Air Raid. The museum is also home to the Japanese Garden of Peace, a gift from the people of Japan to the United States in honor of Adm. Chester W. Nimitz. Visit the museum's website at *www.pacificwarmuseum.org.*

NATIONAL WORLD WAR II MUSEUM

The National World War II Museum in New Orleans, Louisiana, displays and interprets the history of the war through exhibits. Information on the museum can be found at *www.nationalww2museum.org.*

NATIONAL AIR AND SPACE MUSEUM

The Smithsonian Institution's National Air and Space Museum has two facilities, one on the National Mall in Washington, D.C., and a larger aircraft display at the Udvar-Hazy Center in Chantilly, Virginia, adjacent to Dulles International Airport. The National Mall location features galleries on World War II Aviation and Sea-Air Operations that display an A6M Zero fighter as well as an SBD dive bomber and an F4F Wildcat fighter. A number of other Japanese aircraft are on display at the Hazy Center. Details at *www.nasm.org.*

The Pacific Aviation Museum Pearl Harbor displays the remains of Airman First Class Shigenori Nishikaichi's A6M2 Zero BII-120 in an "as found" diorama. His fuel tanks were hit by anti-aircraft fire and Nishikaichi didn't have enough gas to return to Hiryu. He crash landed on the island of Niihau beginning a six-day odyssey that resulted in the Zero being burned, a native Hawaiian being shot by Nishikaichi who in turn was killed by the injured man, and a Japanese worker who had aided Nishikaichi committing suicide. The remains of the wing and engine survived on the island until recovered by the museum in 2006, and the propeller is reportedly on display at Joint Base Pearl Harbor-Hickam. (Photo courtesy Pacific Aviation Museum Pearl Harbor)

BIBLIOGRAPHY

Albright. Harry. *Pearl Harbor Japan's Fatal Blunder: The True Story Behind Japan's Attack on December 7, 1941.* New York. Hippocrene Books, Inc. 1988.

Andrade, John M. *U.S. Military Aircraft Designations and Serials Since 1909.* Earl Shilton, Leicester, England. Midland Counties Publications. 1979.

Arakaki, Leatrice R., and John R. Kuborn. *7 December 1941: The Air Force Story.* Hickam AFB, Hawaii. Office of History, Pacific Air Forces. 1991.

Arroyo, Ernest. *Pearl Harbor.* New York, N.Y. MetroBooks. 2001.

Boyd, Carl, and Akihiko Yoshida. *The Japanese Submarine Force and World War II.* Annapolis, Maryland. Naval Institute Press. 1995.

Browning, Robert M., Jr. *U.S. Merchant Vessel War Casualties of World War II.* Annapolis, Maryland. Naval Institute Press. 1996.

Burlingame, Burl. *Advance Force Pearl Harbor.* Annapolis, Maryland. Naval Institute Press. 1995.

Campbell, Douglas E. *BuNos! Disposition of World War II USN, USMC and USCG Aircraft Listed by Bureau Number.* Syneca Research Group, Inc. Southern Pines, North Carolina. 2012.

Carlson, Elliott, and Rear Adm. Donald "Mac" Showers. *Joe Rochefort's War: The Odyssey of the Codebreaker Who Outwitted Yamamoto at Midway.* Annapolis, Maryland. Naval Institute Press. 2013.

Clausen, Henry C., and Bruce Lee. *Pearl Harbor: Final Judgment.* New York. Crown Publishers, Inc. 1992.

Cohen, Stan. *East Wind Rain: A Pictorial History of the Pearl Harbor Attack.* Missoula, Montana. Pictorial Histories Publishing. 1981.

———. *Attack on Pearl Harbor: A Pictorial History.* Missoula, Montana. Pictorial Histories Publishing. 2001.

Craddock, John. *First Shot: The Untold Story of the Japanese Minisubs That Attacked Pearl Harbor.* New York. McGraw-Hill. 2006.

Cressman, Robert J. *The Official Chronology of the U.S. Navy in World War II.* Annapolis, Maryland. Naval Institute Press. 2000.

Dorr, Robert F. *B-24 Liberator Units of the Pacific War.* Oxford, England. Osprey Publishing, 1999.

Doyle, David. *USS California: A Visual History of the Golden State Battleship BB-44.* Delray Beach, Florida. Ampersand Group, Inc. 2015.

Dull, Paul S. *A Battle History of the Imperial Japanese Navy (1941–1945).* Annapolis, Maryland. Naval Institute Press. 1978.

Francillion, Rene. *Japanese Aircraft of the Pacific War.* Annapolis, Maryland. Naval Institute Press. 1988.

Freeman, Roger, and David Osborne. *The B-17 Flying Fortress Story: Design, Production, History.* London. Arms and Armour Press. 1998.

Gibbs, Jim. *Disaster Log of Ships.* New York, New York: Bonanza Books. 1971.

Goldstein, Donald M., and Katherine V. Dillion. *The Pearl Harbor Papers: Inside the Japanese Plans.* Dulles, Virginia. Brassey's. 1993.

———. *The Pacific War Papers: Japanese Documents of World War II.* Washington, D.C. Potomac Books, Inc. 2004.

Hagedorn, Sr., Dan, and Dan Hagedorn Jr. *The Douglas B-18 and B-23: America's Forsaken Warriors.* Manchester, England. Crécy Publishing Ltd. 2015.

Harding, Stephen. *Voyage to Oblivion: A Sunken Ship, a Vanished Crew, and the Final Myster of Pearl Harbor.* Stroud, Gloucestershire, England. Amberley Publishing. 2010.

Hata, Ikuhiko, Yasuho Izawa (translated by Don Cyril Gorham). *Japanese Naval Aces and Fighter Units in World War II.* Annapolis, Maryland. Naval Institute Press. 1989.

Holmes, W. J. *Double-Edged Secrets. U.S. Naval Intelligence Operations in the Pacific during World War II.* Annapolis, Maryland. Naval Institute Press. 1979.

Horn, Steve. *The Second Attack on Pearl Harbor: Operation K and Other Japanese Attempts to Bomb America in World War II.* Annapolis, Maryland. Naval Institute Press. 2005.

Jones, Syd. *Before and Beyond the Niihau Zero: The Unlikely Drama of Hawaii's Forbidden Island Prior to, During, and After the Pearl Harbor Attack.* Merritt Island, Florida. Signum Ops. 2014.

Kimmett, Larry, and Margaret Regis. *The Attack on Pearl Harbor: An Illustrated History.* Seattle, Washington. Navigator Publishing. 1999.

Lambert, John W. *The Pineapple Air Force: Pearl Harbor to Tokyo.* St. Paul, Minnesota. Phalanx Publishing Co. Ltd. 1990.

Lambert, John W., and Norman Polmar. *Defenseless: Command Failure at Pearl Harbor.* St. Paul, Minnesota. Motorbooks International. 2003.

Larkins, William T. *Battleship and Cruiser Aircraft of the United States Navy, 1910–1949.* Atglen, Pennsylvania. Schiffer Military/Aviation History. 1996.

———. *U.S. Navy Aircraft 1921–1941/U.S. Marine Corps Aircraft 1914–1959.* New York. Crown Publishers Inc. 1988.

Layton, Rear Adm. Edwin T. *"And I Was There" Pearl Harbor and Midway—Breaking the Secrets.* New York. William Morrow and Company, Inc. 1985.

Madsen, Daniel. *Resurrection: Salvaging the Battle Fleet at Pearl Harbor.* Annapolis, Maryland. Naval Institute Press. 2003.

Maloney, Edward T. *Japanese Aircraft Performance and Characteristics (TAIC Manual).* Corona Del Mar, California. Planes of Fame Publications. 1990.

Meek, John Martin. *The Other Pearl Harbor: The Army Air Corps and Its Heroes on Dec. 7, 1941.* Mustang, Oklahoma. Tate Publishing & Enterprises, LLC. 2011.

Miller, Edward S. *War Plan Orange: The U.S. Strategy to Defeat Japan 1897–1945.* Annapolis, Maryland. Naval Institute Press. 1991.

Morrison, Samuel Eliot. *The Two-Ocean War: A Short History of the United States Navy in the Second World War.* Boston, Massachusetts. Atlantic-Little, Brown. 1963.

———. *History of United States Naval Operations in World War II.* Vols. 1–15. Boston, Massachusetts. Atlantic-Little, Brown. 1948–1968.

Orita, Zenji, with Joseph D. Harrington. *I-Boat Captain: How Japan's Submarines Almost Defeated the U.S. Navy in the Pacific!* Canoga Park, California. Major Books. 1976.

Phister, Jeff, with Thomas Hone and Paul Goodyear. *Battleship Oklahoma BB-37.* Norman, Oklahoma. University of Oklahoma Press. 2008.

Prange, Gordon W. *At Dawn We Slept: The Untold Story of Pearl Harbor.* New York. Penguin Books. 1981.

———. *Miracle at Midway.* New York. McGraw Hill. 1982.

———. *Pearl Harbor: The Verdict of History.* New York. McGraw Hill. 1986.

Raymer, Edward C. *Descent into Darkness: Pearl Harbor, 1941—A Navy Diver's Memoir.* Novato, California. Presidio Press. 1996.

Sakaida, Henry. *Imperial Japanese Navy Aces 1937–1945.* Botley, Oxford, England. Osprey Publishing Ltd. 1998.

Sherrod, Robert. *History of Marine Corps Aviation in World War II.* Baltimore, Maryland. The Nautical and Aviation Publishing Company of America. 1987.

Slackman, Michael. *Remembering Pearl Harbor: The Story of the U.S.S. Arizona Memorial.* Honolulu, Hawaii. Arizona Memorial Museum Association. 1984.

Smith, Carl. *Pearl Harbor.* Botley, Oxford, England. Osprey Publishing. 2001.

Smith, Michael. *The Emperor's Codes: The Breaking of Japan's Secret Ciphers.* New York. Arcade Publishing. 2000.

Stillwell, Paul. *Air Raid Pearl Harbor: Recollections of a Day of Infamy.* Annapolis, Maryland. Naval Institute Press. 1981.

Tagaya, Osamu. *Aichi 99 Kanbaku "Val" Units 1937–1942.* Long Island City, New York. Osprey Publishing Ltd. 2011.

Theobald, Rear Adm. Robert A. *The Final Secret of Pearl Harbor: The Washington Contribution to the Japanese Attack.* Old Greenwich, Connecticut. The Devin-Adair Company. 1954.

Thorpe, Brig. Gen. Elliott R. *East Wind, Rain: The Intimate Account of an Intelligence Officer in the Pacific 1939–1949.* Boston, Massachusetts. Gambit Inc. 1969.

Unknown. *Ships in Gray: The Story of Matson in World War II.* San Francisco, California. Matson Navigation Co. 1946.

Veronico, Nicholas A. *Hidden Warships: Finding World War II's Abandoned, Sunk, and Preserved Warships.* St. Paul, Minnesota. Zenith Press. 2015.

———. *Hidden Warbirds: The Epic Stories of Finding, Recovering, and Rebuilding WWII's Lost Aircraft.* St. Paul, Minnesota. Zenith Press. 2013.

————. *Hidden Warbirds II: More Epic Stories of Finding, Recovering, and Rebuilding WWII's Lost Aircraft.* St. Paul, Minnesota. Zenith Press. 2014.

————. *Images of America: World War II Shipyards by the Bay.* Charleston, South Carolina. Arcadia Publishing. 2007.

Veronico, Nicholas A., and Armand H. Veronico. *Battlestations: American Warships of World War II in Color.* Osceola, Wisconsin. Motorbooks International. 2001.

Wallin, Homer N. *Pearl Harbor: Why, How, Fleet Salvage and Final Appraisal.* Washington, D.C. Naval History Division. U.S. Government Printing Office. 1968.

Webber, Bert. *Silent Siege III: Japanese Attacks on North America in World War II.* Medford, Oregon: Webb Research Group. 1992.

Wenger, J. Michael, Robert J. Cressman, and John F. Di Virgilio. *No One Avoided Danger: NAS Kaneohe Bay and the Japanese Attack of 7 December 1941.* Annapolis, Maryland. Naval Institute Press. 2015.

Williford, Glen. *Racing the Sunrise: Reinforcing America's Pacific Outposts, 1941–1942.* Annapolis, Maryland. Naval Institute Press. 2010.

Young. Stephen Bower. *Trapped at Pearl Harbor: Escape from Battleship Oklahoma.* Annapolis, Maryland. Naval Institute Press. 1991.

GOVERNMENT PUBLICATIONS

Air University. *USAF Credits for the Destruction of Enemy Aircraft, World War II.* Maxwell AFB, Alabama. 1978.

Department of Defense. *The "Magic" Background of Pearl Harbor.* Vols. 1-5. Washington, D.C. U.S. Government Printing Office. 1977.

Navy Department, Office of the Chief of Naval Operations. *Dictionary of American Naval Fighting Ships.* Vols. 1–8. Washington, D.C. U.S. Government Printing Office. 1959–1977.

Navy Department, Department of Ordnance and Gunnery. *Naval Ordnance and Gunnery, Vol. I: Naval Ordnance.* Washington, D.C. U.S. Government Printing Office. 1955.

U.S. Senate. *Investigation of the Pearl Harbor Attack: Report of the Joint Committee on the Investigation of the Pearl Harbor Attack.* Washington, D.C. U.S. Government Printing Office. 1946.

U.S. Senate. *Investigation of the Pearl Harbor Attack: Hearings Before the Joint Committee on the Investigation of the Pearl Harbor Attack.* Washington, D.C. U.S. Government Printing Office. 1946. Parts 1–38.

U.S. Strategic Bombing Survey (Pacific). *The Campaigns of the Pacific War.* Washington, D.C. U.S. Government Printing Office. 1946.

U.S. Strategic Bombing Survey (Naval Analysis Division). *Interrogations of Japanese Officials.* Vols. I and II. Washington, D.C. U.S. Government Printing Office. 1946.

REPORTS/DOCUMENTS

Baldwin, Lt. C. B. *Crash of Enemy Plane on Niihau.* Fourteenth Naval District Branch Intelligence Office. Dec. 16, 1941. National Archives at San Francisco, RG 181.

Baughman, C. C. (Captain of the Yard, Navy Yard, Pearl Harbor, Territory of Hawaii). *Report on Japanese Air Attack on Pearl Harbor on December 7, 1941.* Dec. 20, 1941. National Archives at San Francisco, RG 181.

Commander Destroyer Division Eighty. Attacks by Japanese of December 7; report on participation by Destroyer Division Eighty. Dec. 12, 1941. National Archives at San Francisco, RG 181.

Commanding Officer, U.S.S. *Ward. Sinking of a Japanese Submarine by U.S.S. Ward.* Dec. 13, 1941. National Archives at San Francisco, RG 181.

Martin, H. M. (Commanding Officer, Naval Air Station, Kaneohe Bay, Territory of Hawaii). *The incidents connected with the air raid at the Naval Air Station, Kaneohe Bay, T.H. on 7 December 1941— Narrative of.* National Archives at San Francisco, RG 181.

Miller, D. B. (Commanding Officer, U.S.S. *Allen*— DD-66). Air Raid Attack by Japanese—Report on. Dec. 14, 1941. National Archives at San Francisco, RG 181.

Mizuha, First Lt. Jack H. *Report of Events Since Sunday, 7 December, 1941, on Niihau.* U.S. Army, 299th Infantry. National Archives at San Francisco, RG 181. Undated.

Shannon, H.D. (Commanding Officer, Defense Garrison, Fleet Marine Force, Midway Islands). *Report of action on night of 7 December, 1941.* Dec. 12, 1941. National Archives at San Francisco, RG 181.

PERIODICALS

Aiken, David. "Hirano's Zero: A Mitsubishi Zero shot down at Pearl Harbor Revealed surprisingly few facts about the mysterious fighter, but did yield a map that provided tantalizing clues about the location of the Japanese Fleet." *Aviation History.* January 2009.

————. "Pearl Harbor's Lost P-36: Still Missing After 60 Years—2nd Lt. Gordon Sterling." *Flight Journal.* October 2002.

Birdsall, Steve. "Pacific Tramps: The Story of the B-17s That Arrived Over Hawaii During the Japanese Attack Has Been Told Many Times, But What Happened to Them?" *Aviation History.* May 2016.

"Jap Subs Off Coast: Three Dead, Five Missing In Four Raids." *San Francisco Chronicle*, Dec. 23, 1941.

Needam, Howard. "Captain Tells Own Story of Sub Raid." *San Francisco Chronicle*, Dec. 22, 1941.

"S.F. Sub Attack: Survivors Tell Gripping Story How U.S. Pilots Battled Raider." *San Francisco Chronicle*, Dec. 23, 1941.

"Ship Sunk Dec. 7 Was S.F. Owned." *San Francisco Chronicle*, Dec. 20, 1941.

"The Sub Stories: Attacks on U.S. Freighters Occurred Off Santa Cruz, Eureka; One Ship In Port." *San Francisco Chronicle*, Dec. 21, 1941.

"Three U.S. Ships Missing In The Pacific." *San Francisco Chronicle*, Dec. 8, 1941.

ACKNOWLEDGMENTS

Pearl Harbor, its aftermath, as well as the veterans of the attack and those who served our nation were exceedingly real to me growing up. Many people I met were combat veterans, including a number of my school teachers; listening to their uncensored stories, meeting Pearl Harbor survivors, and seeing the memorial spanning the hull of the *Arizona* were all moving experiences. Some people lived with the war every day, my late father-in-law had two ships sunk from under him by the Japanese, and he was still bitter more than forty years after the war.

That said, the time has passed to put the bitterness behind us. Every day is a day to remember the men and women who served and those who made the ultimate sacrifice—on both sides of the conflict.

Preparing this book benefited greatly with valuable conversations, exchange of information, and insight to the conflict shared by Pearl Harbor historians and authors David Aiken, Ernest Arroyo, David Trojan, and Craig Fuller of Aircraft Archaeological Investigation and Research. Carol Wilson from the National Archives and Records Administration, Sierra Nevada Region provided excellent access to the Sierra Nevada Region's photography collection. Special thanks to David Reisch from Stackpole Books for the opportunity to present this work. I also want to thank: Ian Abbott, Caroline and Ray Bingham, Steve Birdsall, Claire and Joe Bradshaw, Roger Cain, Ed Davies, Jim Dunn, Wayne Gomes, Kevin Grantham, Ted Holgerson, William T. Larkins, Dale Messimer, Stan Piet, Taigh Ramey, Lee Scales, Doug Scroggins, Ron Strong, Scott Thompson, Rick Turner, Armand and Karen Veronico, Betty Veronico, Kathleen and Tony Veronico. Thank you all.

A word about Appendix D, U.S. Navy Aircraft Destroyed, December 7, 1941, and Appendix E, U.S. Army Air Forces Aircraft Destroyed, December 7, 1941: Both are as accurate as they can be at the time of publication. Record keeping in the opening days of the war was chaotic at best, and each service's records are quite different in the amount of detail recorded for each aircraft. For example, some of the Wheeler Field-based P-40s were destroyed at Hickam Field, but with the records at hand, there is no way to determine which aircraft were destroyed whereas only the squadron of record is listed, not the location of loss. Often the only indication on the record card is "lost 12-7-41." The answer may lie in the tower records of Hickam Field for the day or days preceding the attack, but those have yet to turn up. There are also photos of aircraft that appear to be damaged beyond repair, but their record card indicates service in subsequent years. The author welcomes updates, corrections with definitive records, photos, and any new information to improve these lists.

Nicholas A. Veronico
San Carlos, California